STE'

CW00369467

Foreword by
Lady Claire Macdonald

I feel so privileged to be invited to write this foreword. This Guide is the best. Alan Stevenson has collated exactly what is required by all seeking guidance on where to stay or eat in Scotland. He seeks out the top quality, and his values are those so sought after by those visiting Scotland as well as by those of us who love to travel and discover new parts of this wonderful country.

My emphasis is always on food. Within Scotland, both mainland and islands, the best food in the world is raised, produced, grown, or caught – in the case of those who fish the seas around Scotland as well as the freshwater rivers and lochs. And Scotland is also producing an increasingly growing band of chefs skilled in the cooking of this wonderful food. There are Scots to be found cooking in all the best places to eat up and down Great Britain, as well as here at home in Scotland. These skills are essential to show-case the top quality food from Scotland. The Stevenson Guide displays just where to find such outstanding food cooked by these exceptional chefs.

A Guide is such a concentration of endeavour to produce. I would like to pay tribute here to Alan Stevenson for executing such a Guide of excellence again this year. And to thank him for it. It deserves to knock all the other Guides off the shelves!

Claire Macdonald
Kinloch Lodge,
Sleat, Isle of Skye

FOREWORD

STEVENSONS

SCOTLAND'S
GOOD HOTEL AND FOOD BOOK
2013

Published by:
Alan Stevenson Publications
Fala
20 West Cairn Crescent
Penicuik
Midlothian
EH26 0AR
Tel: 01968 678015
Mobile: 07786 966341
Email: alan@stevensons-scotland.com
www.stevensons-scotland.com

North American Representative:
Ann Litt,
Undiscovered Britain
11978 Audubon Place
Philadelphia, PA 19116
Tel: (215) 969-0542
Fax: (215) 969-9251
Email: annlitt413@gmail.com
www:UndiscoveredBritain.com

Consultant: James Chassels

Copyright © 2012 Stevensons - Scotland's Good Hotel and Food Book - Eighteenth Edition

ISBN 978-0-9550877-7-6

Price: £10.00
$18.00 from USA agent only. (Includes Canada)
See page 94 for price list plus postage & packaging

Typesetting/Graphics: Colin Shepherd.
Proof Administration: Katie Fenton of Aviemore Business Solutions.
Printed in Scotland: J. Thomson Colour Printers, Glasgow.
Front Cover: Rocpool Reserve & Chez Roux, City of Inverness, Inverness-shire.

Alan Stevenson
Publisher

Delighted to welcome you all to **STEVENSONS 2013** *– the* **18th edition** *of Scotland's Good Hotel & Food Book.*

The year 2012 has proved to be a difficult trading year for many with extreme weather conditions, the recession, fuel costs and even the Olympics cited as the main reasons. Visitor numbers were down again with Aberdeenshire (oil related business) and the island properties 'bucking the trend'. There has been no pattern to the season hence bookings were described as 'up and down'. June and July were very disappointing.

My personal collection once again includes hotels and restaurants which reflect the very best of Scottish hospitality. Very few casualties which I could not include for various reasons and a few new entries which have made the 'grade' or I have been keeping an eye on over the years (Tor-Na-Coille in Banchory an example). Kinloch Lodge on Skye (see food entry) are celebrating their 40th anniversary and I was delighted Lady Claire Macdonald penned the Main Foreword for me (Page 1). Also a very talented young chef, Derek Johnstone from Greywalls & Chez Roux who penned the Food Foreword for me.

My newsletter on pages 10 and 11 provides more information on items of interest within the industry. It's a general update – staff appointments, awards, etc. On pages 12 and 13 you will find my 'Roll of Honour'. This well deserved accolade marks the achievement of people I have worked with over 25 years. Many will be known to my readers.

Grateful to my sponsors for their continued support and as always I look forward to my travels next year when I will compile the **19th edition** *of the book for year 2014.*

INTRODUCTION

3 STEVENSONS 2013   Photo by Yerbury of Edinburgh

STEVENSONS

SCOTLAND'S
GOOD HOTEL AND FOOD BOOK
2013

CONTENTS   PAGE

Trade Sponsors

We do not use growth hormones in any shape or form.

The Scotch Beef Club is unashamedly based on quality.

We offer independent assurance, supported by the Scottish SPCA.

Our members believe strongly in animal welfare.

Our standards are much higher than legislation demands.

Fresh meat is low in salt and high in iron.

Our members are passionate about red meat.

Less stressed animals provide better tasting meat.

We are supported by some of the UK's finest chefs.

Cattle are reared mainly outdoors and fed on a grass diet.

All our livestock are born and raised for all of their lives on assured farms in Scotland.

Modern breeding and butchery standards produce leaner meat.

Looking for a reason to try a Scotch Beef club restaurant?

Well, here's twelve.

Our member restaurants are a cut above the rest. That's why they choose the finest Scotch Beef. With full traceability and guaranteed levels of assurance, Scotch Beef is high on quality, high on taste. So if you care about your food, look for the Scotch Beef Club logo on your next meal out. We can think of at least a dozen reasons why.

 Look out for the member restaurants throughout this guide wherever you see this symbol.

SCOTCH BEEF

PROTECTED GEOGRAPHICAL INDICATION

THE SCOTCH BEEF CLUB

To find a member restaurant near you, visit: **www.scotchbeefclub.org**

STEVENSONS

SCOTLAND'S
GOOD HOTEL AND FOOD BOOK
2013

AWARDS/SYMBOLS

VisitScotland (Scottish Tourist Board)

The Star System is a world-first. It denotes quality assurance on a range of 1 to 5 stars. This is why it is only the quality of the welcome and service, the food, the hospitality, ambience and the comfort and condition of the property which earns VisitScotland stars, not the size of the accommodation or the range of facilities. Gold stars recognise businesses which constantly achieve the hightest level of excellence within their VisitScotland star rating. This business has excelled in the areas of customer care and hospitality and displays evidence of a real commitment to staff development and training.

The quality grades awarded are, eg:

GOLD

★★★★★	Exceptional, world-class
★★★★	Excellent
★★★	Very Good
★★	Good

AA Red Rosettes

Hotels and restaurants may be awarded red rosettes to denote the quality of food they serve. It is an award scheme, not a classification scheme. They award rosettes annually on a rising scale of one to five.

AA Red Stars ★★★★★

The AA top hotels in Britain and Ireland are assessed and announced annually with a red star award. They recognise the very best hotels in the country that offer consistently outstanding levels of quality, comfort, cleanliness and comfort care. Red stars are awarded on a rising scale of one to five. Restaurants with rooms also qualify for this award.

Bull Logo

Any establishment which displays the Bull Logo is a member of the Scotch Beef Club. The criteria is strict - the product is derived from cattle born, reared for all of their lives, slaughtered and dressed in Scotland. The animals will have been produced in accordance with assurance schemes accredited to European Standard and meeting the standards and assessments set by Quality Meat Scotland's Assurance Schemes.

PLEASE NOTE: THESE AWARDS DO NOT NECESSARILY FORM PART OF MY OVERALL PERSONAL SELECTION OF GOOD HOTELS AND RESTAURANTS IN SCOTLAND. THEY ARE INCLUDED TO ASSIST THE VISITOR SELECT HIS/HER HOTEL OR RESTAURANT OF CHOICE. THE AWARDS ARE NOT MANDATORY FOR SELECTION TO THIS PUBLICATION.

THE ROYAL EDINBURGH MILITARY TATTOO

CASTELLUM EST URBS

2-24 August
2013

2013 highlights Scotland's reputation as a land of outstanding beauty as the Tattoo celebrates the Year of Natural Scotland.

The programme will include all the famed music, action and colour with a soupçon of the unexpected, featuring performers from all points of the compass including the Far East, Europe as well as Central and South America.

With the Massed Pipes and Drums, Military Bands, display teams, dancers and the haunting lament of the Lone Piper set against the magnificent backcloth of Edinburgh Castle.

Tickets available December 2012
Tel: +44(0)131 225 1188   Fax: +44(0)131 225 8627
Email: tickets@edintattoo.co.uk

www.edintattoo.co.uk
The Tattoo Office 32 Market Street
Edinburgh EH1 1QB Scotland

One **Voice**,
One **Celebration**

STEVENSONS

SCOTLAND'S
GOOD HOTEL AND FOOD BOOK
2013

HOW TO LOCATE A HOTEL OR RESTAURANT

1. First look at the map of **Scotland on page 14.** The place name of the hotels or restaurants I am featuring will be highlighted in bold type. Restaurants will be highlighted with a red circle. ●

2. Once you have pinpointed your location *follow along the top of the pages*, which are arranged alphabetically, until you arrive at your location.

3. If you already have the name of the hotel or restaurant and wish to know if it is included, turn to the index at the back of the book. Hotels and restaurants are listed alphabetically.

4. In some cases where hotels and restaurants are located close to major towns, they may be shown under that town with the exact location in brackets. For example, **FORT WILLIAM (Torlundy).**

5. **Hotel Price guide:** This quote is based on an overnight stay single & double. Normally this is for bed & breakfast but sometimes if dinner is included it will be indicated. (includes dinner). Also applicable to restaurants with rooms.

Rocpool & Chez Roux

6. The above prices are quoted for a one night stay, but most of the establishments in this book offer reductions for stays of two or more nights. Also please enquire about seasonal bargain 'breaks'.

7. **Symbols/Awards.** Awards from VisitScotland (Quality Assurance Classification), AA red food rosettes & stars and the Bull Logo (Scotch Beef Club - Quality Meat Scotland) appear on hotel and restaurant entries. See introductory pages for a full explanation of these symbols and awards.

STEVENSONS

General News

Forecasted in my report last year **Inver Lodge & Chez Roux** have been awarded VisitScotland 5 star status. Congratulations to all. **Gordon, Maria & Garry Watson** at **Gordon's Restaurant**, Inverkeilor by Arbroath have been awarded 3 AA rosettes. **Darin Campbell, Hotel Du Vin** at One Devonshire Gardens has been awarded 3 AA rosettes. **Margaret Jaffray** has retired after 45 years at **Banchory Lodge Hotel**. **Lady Claire & Lord Godfrey Macdonald** (and family) are celebrating 4 decades at **Kinloch Lodge** on the Isle of Skye (buy the new book!) The **Atholl** and **Rocpool Apartments** in Edinburgh and **Alladale Wilderness Lodge & Reserve** north of Inverness (Ardgay) have been added to the **Inverlochy Castle Management International** portfolio (ICMI). See entries for further details. **Phillip Fleming**, known to me from his early days at **Inverlochy Castle** is now General Manager of **Tor-Na-Coille Hotel** in Banchory

Marcliffe Hotel, Restaurant & Spa

Culloden House Hotel

(see entry in book). **The Torridon** have won the AA Scottish Hotel of the Year 2012-2013. The **MacCallum Family** celebrate 55 years at **Glengarry Castle**.

STAFF APPOINTMENTS & ACTIVITY

Jody Marshall (ex **The Summer Isles Hotel**) and **Scott Scorer** (ex **Gleneagles**) have been appointed, respectively, as General Manager and Head Chef at **Ballathie House**. **Mark Slaney** has been appointed General Manager at **The Horseshoe Inn**, Eddleston, near Peebles. He was formerly at **Ackergill Tower, Boath House** and **Isle of Eriska**. **Riad Peerbux**, a native of Mauritius, has been appointed head chef at **The Horseshoe Inn**. **Robbie** and **Maggs Cairns** (ex **Flodigarry** on Skye) have bought **Fortingall House Hotel** near Aberfeldy in Perthshire. **Kildrummy Castle** is now operated by **Claude S Berquier** and **Elise Schawlb** from France arriving via Dubai. **Christopher Firth-Bernard**, who held a Michelin Star for many years, has left **The Summer Isles Hotel**. **Robert MacPherson** has left his post as head chef of **Airds Hotel** in Appin (formerly **Isle of Eriska** for many years). **David Mutter**, head chef at **Darroch Learg** has been replaced by his sous chef **John Jeremiah**. **Walter Walker**, after 22 years as head chef at **Bunchrew House Hotel**, Inverness has been appointed head chef at **Meldrum House Hotel & Country Club**, Aberdeenshire.

STEVENSONS

ROLL OF HONOUR

As one can imagine, over the past 30 years, I have met many people in my travels and although there is the business element to my annual publication it could be viewed as a 'family' of hotels and restaurants. Many are now very good friends. I have come to know their children, some of who have taken over from their parents – and now even their grandchildren! I still maintain friendships with some who have retired. There are a number who have devoted themselves to this industry and I have listed below a number of people who have 'lasted the pace' and should be recognised for their long, and should I add, distinguished service. Pity there's not a medal for this 'award'.

OVER 25 YEARS SERVICE

Frances Malcolm:
Administration, **Kingsmills Hotel**, Inverness.
Bill Sloan:
Concierge, **Kingsmills Hotel**, Inverness.
Henrietta Fergusson:
Killiecrankie House Hotel, Perthshire.
Jane Watson:
General Manager, **Inverlochy Castle**, Fort William.
Michael Leonard:
Inverlochy Castle, Fort William (retired).
Margaret Jaffray:
Banchory Lodge Hotel, Banchory (retired 2012).
The Spence Family:
Marcliffe Hotel, Restaurant & Spa, Aberdeen.
Michael Simpson:
Head Chef, **Culloden House**, Inverness.
The Quinion Family:
Farlam Hall (England Associate Hotel).
Kenneth Charleson:
Marketing Director, **Hebridean Princess.**

Nicholas Gorton:
> General Manager, **Inver Lodge Hotel & Chez Roux**, Lochinver.

Grace Stuart:
> Housekeeper, **Inver Lodge Hotel & Chez Roux**, Lochinver.

The MacCallum Family:
> **Glengarry Castle**, Invergarry, Inverness-shire.

Garry Dinnes:
> **Ramnee Hotel**, Forres & Inverness City Suites.

Harrison Family:
> **Pool House, Poolewe**, Wester Ross.

The Brown Family:
> **Roman Camp Country House**, Callander, Stirlingshire.

Lady Claire & Lord Godfrey Macdonald & Family:
> **Kinloch Lodge**, Sleat, Isle of Skye.

Shirley & Eddie Spears:
> **The Three Chimneys**, Colbost, Isle of Skye.

Lewis Family:
> **Monachyle Mhor**, Balquhidder, Perthshire.

Gordon & Cherry Gunn:
> **Creagan House**, Strathyre, Perthshire.

Alan & Joyce Craigie & family:
> **The Creel Restaurant**, Orkney.

David & Mary Allen:
> **Steadings at The Grouse & Trout**, Flichity, Inverness-shire.

Allen Family:
> **Kinloch House**, Blairgowrie, Perthshire.

Rohaise Rose-Bristow (nee Gregory):
> **The Torridon**, Wester Ross.

Nigel & Fiona Franks:
> **Darroch Learg**, Ballater, Aberdeenshire.

If I have omitted any names I apologise. Its quite a 'roll of honour' and my regular readers will know most of the names listed.

ROLL OF HONOUR

THE MARCLIFFE HOTEL, SPA AND RESTAURANT

North Deeside Road, Aberdeen. AB15 9YA
Tel: 01224 861000   Fax: 01224 868860
Email: reservations@marcliffe.com   www.marcliffe.com

My association with the Spence family spans 25 years and I always look forward to my visits here. Truly a wonderful 5 star experience where one can savour the delights of consistently high standards of hotel-keeping. I spent four nights here throughout the year and enjoyed every minute. Most of the staff have been here for years and I know most of them now by their first names. Great ambience prevails throughout. The hotel is well positioned on the Deeside Road in the attractive suberb of Cults – magnificent setting in 11 acres of woodland and garden policies with ample car parking. Bedroom suites are large and complete with quality furnishings and all modern facilities one would expect such as satellite TV, modem points and mini bar. Public areas, with roaring log fires (when required) are extremely comfortable. Menu includes Scottish lobster and Russian King Crab. Wine cellar of note to match and bar stocked with over 100 malt whiskies. Perfect base to explore the castle & whisky trails – even as far as Balmoral Castle. Gymnasium and beauty spa offering a selection of treatments. Testament to the hard work of the Spence family over many years. Member of Small Luxury Hotels Of The World and Connoisseurs Scotland.

Open: *All year*	**Gymnasium/Beauty Spa:** *Yes (see above)*
No. Rooms: *42 En Suite 42*	**Conference Facilities:** *Extremely good*
Room telephones: *Yes*	**Price Guide:** *Single £150.00 - £350.00 (suite)*
TV in Rooms: *Yes*	*Double £160.00 - £350.00 (suite)*
Pets: *Yes* **Children:** *Yes*	**Location:** *Aberdeen ring road, turn west at A93 - to Braemar.*
Disabled: *Yes*	*Hotel is 1ml on right. Aberdeen airport 25mins.*

David Littlewood - Head Chef
Raemoir House Hotel

RAEMOIR HOUSE HOTEL

Nr. Banchory, Aberdeenshire. AB31 4ED
Tel: 01330 824884

Email: hotel@raemoir.com www.raemoir.com

This is a magnificent property – the approach through the main gateway and treelined driveway to the main building is very impressive. This regal Georgian mansion is situated in wide parkland a mile to the north of Banchory in easy reach of Aberdeen and Royal Deeside. Part of the house dates from 1715 but the main house was built in 1817. Over the years the house has been transformed into one of Scotland's premier country houses. There are 14 majestic bedrooms (& en suite facilities) with every comfort one would expect and a further 6 'cosy' bedrooms in the older building known as the Ha' House. Exceptional views over fields and woodland. Public rooms spacious and extremely comfortable with roaring log fires. The food and beverage operation here are quite exceptional. The talents of executive chef David Littlewood are obvious allied with a first class front of house operation. A plethora of awards have come as no surprise. I can assure you, diners' expectations are fully met. Great ambience whether dining formally in the dining room or relaxing in the spacious bar area. Conference and wedding enquiries welcome. Your hosts: Mr. and Mrs. Neil Rae; General Manager: Elaine Maitland. Highly recommended.

Open: *All year*	**Disabled:** *Limited*
No. Rooms: *20 En Suite 20*	**Conference Facilities:** *60 delegates*
Room telephones: *Yes*	**Price Guide:** *Single from £105.00*
TV in Rooms: *Yes*	*Double from £150.00*
Pets: *By arrangement*	**Location:** *Mile north of Banchory*
Children: *Yes*	

Mark De Freitas - Head Chef
Lake of Menteith - Hotel and Restaurant

LAKE OF MENTEITH
(HOTEL & WATERFRONT RESTAURANT)
Port of Menteith, Perthshire. FK8 3RA
Tel: 01877 385258
Email: enquiries@lake-hotel.com www.lake-hotel.com

This hotel is situated in the most idyllic and picturesque position one could wish for – right beside the only Lake in Scotland. The 'image' and interior of this hotel have been transformed in recent years from what I remember. Decorated in the warm and welcoming style of a classic New England waterfront hotel, with muted tones and the extensive use of local timber and stone in the restaurant and bar. All rooms have been extensively upgraded with care and attention to detail - rooms with lake views are 'out of this world' with all modern amenities and nice personal touches. The comfort of the guest is paramount. In addition to the discerning traveller, the Lake Hotel will provide facilities for small corporate meetings and exclusive weddings, whilst the food and beverage operation is one of the best in the country. The waterfront restaurant serves seasonal, local produce thoughtfully and imaginatively prepared. Proprietor Ian Fleming has really 'turned' this hotel around and it is a major player within the country house scene. Has all the attributes of a first class operation in a very attractive setting. Only a short drive from Glasgow or Edinburgh.

Open: *All year*	**Swimming Pool/Health Club:** *No*
No. Rooms: *17*	**Conference Facilities:** *24 Director level*
Room telephones: *Yes*	**Price Guide:** *Single £68.00 Double £90.00 – £225.00*
TV in Rooms: *Yes*	**Location:** *Turn off M9 at Junct. 10 onto A84, follow to A873*
Pets: *No* **Children:** *Yes*	*signposted Aberfoyle. On to Port of Menteith then*
Disabled: *Yes*	*left down the B8034. Hotel 250 yds on right.*

AA ❀ ❀

Join one of our **active and creative courses** in a beautiful, inspiring location, with excellent tutors, delicious home-cooked food and comfortable accommodation.

Or **take a cottage**; relax with your family, explore the island's rich history and wildlife, play in boats and revel in the space and wildness.

Isle of Tanera Mòr
Summer Isles

WEAVING WILDLIFE KAYAKING ART WRITING COTTAGES COURSES BOATS CAFE & POST OFFICE

Just 45 minutes from Ullapool and 15 minutes in our ferryboat, Patricia

www.summer-isles.com   **01854 622 252**   **lizzie@summer-isles.com**

ALLADALE WILDERNESS RESERVE

Ardgay, Sutherland. IV24 3BS
Tel: 01463 716416

Email: enquiries@alladale.co.uk www.alladale.co.uk www.icmi.co.uk

Aptly named this 23,000 acre estate offers luxury and seclusion in a truly magnificent Scottish Highland setting only an hour's drive from Inverness. The journey alone adds to the anticipation. You will not be disappointed. What can only be described as a unique experience the main Lodge offers exclusive use for up to 14 people in 7 en suite bedrooms and is fully staffed. Ideal for that special family occasion or for interest groups/corporate meetings. Quality furnishings and fittings throughout in keeping with the high standards of Inverlochy Castle Management International who manage the property. Outstanding menus produced by the renowned Albert Roux OBE, KFO who is head of the famous cooking dynasty behind such establishments as Le Gavroche which was the first ever restaurant in the UK to be awarded three Michelin Stars. The Eagles Crag Lodge & Ghillie's Rest Lodge offer luxury self catering for up to 8 and 4 guests respectively. Breakfast pack provided – packed lunches and suppers can be provided. Outdoor activities include pony trekking, fishing, stalking, mountain biking, clay pigeon shooting and golf at nearby Dornoch. Idyllic retreat with spectacular views and a few birds of prey overhead! Complete luxury.

Open: *All year*	**Conference Facilities:** *Yes*	
No. Rooms: *Main: 7; Ghillies: 2; Eagles: 3*	**Price Guide:** *Main Lodge: £2,300.00 - £3,300.00 per night*	
TV in Rooms: *Yes*	*Eagles Crag Lodge: £900.00 - £1,300.00 per night*	
Pets: *By arrangement*	*Ghillie's Rest Lodge: £450.00 - £650.00 per night*	
Children: *Yes* **Disabled:** *Main Lodge*	**Location:**	*A9 north from Inverness, B9176 before Alness to Ardgay.*
Swimming Pool/Health Club: *No*		*Left at the building named Alladale Wilderness Reserve.*

THE EISENHOWER @ CULZEAN CASTLE
Culzean Castle
Maybole, Ayrshire. KA19 8LE
Tel: 01655 884455 Fax: 01655 884503
email: culzean@nts.org.uk www.eisenhowerculzean.co.uk

Culzean Castle, a National Trust for Scotland property, is located on the west coast of Scotland 12 miles south of Ayr. Its unrivalled position perched on a cliff top, with magnificent sea views, is spectacular. Hidden away at the top of the Castle is The Eisenhower, a country house style hotel, which is available all year round and offers six individually styled rooms and suites. The Eisenhower was once the relaxing retreat of President Eisenhower, having been gifted to him by the Kennedy family. It is now the ideal venue for a relaxing break or a special occasion where you can enjoy all that its location has to offer – close to championship golf courses at Turnberry and Troon. Guests can use the spectacular Round Drawing Room, with fabulous views across to Arran, and the cosy Dining Room, which has views to Ailsa Craig, is ideal for a romantic dinner for 2 or a larger family gathering. For that special gathering the Eisenhower can also be hired for exclusive use to host celebrations including small intimate weddings. Overnight stay here on two occasions - delightful experience.

Open: *All year*	**Swimming Pool/Health Club:** *No*
No. Rooms: *6*	**Conference Facilities:** *Up to 90*
Room telephones: *No*	**Price Guide:** *Single £150.00 – £250.00 Double £225.00 – £375.00*
TV in Rooms: *No*	**Location:** *From Glasgow M77/A77 towards Ayr. Within 1*
Pets: *No* **Children:** *Yes*	*hour of Glasgow airports. Castle is 12 miles south*
Disabled: *Limited*	*of Ayr on A719. Maybole train station 4 miles.*

DARROCH LEARG HOTEL & RESTAURANT

Braemar Road, Ballater, Royal Deeside, Aberdeenshire. AB35 5UX
Tel: 013397 55443 Fax: 013397 55252
Email: enquiries@darrochlearg.co.uk www.darrochlearg.co.uk

A magnificent country mansion perched above the village with wonderful views across the valley. This mansion house has been the home of the Franks family for many years and a very relaxed and friendly atmosphere prevails – really a home from home except you can expect a bit of pampering and comfort. Elegance is the word I would use when I stayed here – traits of a more graceful era with the family being an integral part of the experience. Delightful and spacious bedrooms, some with great views and some 4 posters. Drawing room and cosy nook with log fires offer every comfort. This hotel has one of the best restaurants in the area and is known for its culinary delights. One could even say that the business is food driven. Dinner is served in a spacious conservatory setting with a wonderful outlook over the hills. The seabass with a chive veloute was a culinary triumph in itself. Obviously a dedicated approach here with sound technical skills and the diners expectations fully met. Wine cellar of note. With canapes and petit fours this is good value for money at £45.00. Over the years Nigel and Fiona Franks have certainly created 'something special' – certainly not commonplace and not to be missed. Not far from Balmoral Castle this is an area of outstanding scenery, fine walks with the castle and whisky trails a favourite.

Open: *All year exc. Xmas week & 3 wks Jan.*	**Disabled:** *Category 3. 1 room floor level*
No. Rooms: *12 En Suite 12*	**Swimming Pool/Health Club:** *No*
Room telephones: *Yes*	**Conference Facilities:** *12 Director Level*
TV in Rooms: *Yes*	**Price Guide:** *Double £140.00 - £250.00 (Master)*
Pets: *Yes*	**Location:** *On A93 at the western end of Ballater on road*
Children: *Yes*	*to Braemar*

MONACHYLE MHOR

Balquhidder, Lochearnhead, Perthshire. FK19 8PQ
Tel: 01877 384622 Fax: 01877 384305
Email: info@monachylemhor.com www.monachylemhor.com

If you require a rural and romantic destination allied with comfort, service and excellent cuisine head for Monachyle Mhor at Balquhidder. Only 4 miles from the village itself this property enjoys a spectacular position overlooking Loch Voil and Loch Doine. The estate itself covers 2000 acres and is the domain of Tom Lewis (chef/proprietor) His culinary skills are well known - using fresh produce from the estate or his own organic garden Tom produces dishes which demonstrate complete dedication. Bedrooms are extremely comfortable with all modern amenities. Courtyard cottages with wood burning stoves offer an attractive option, centrally heated with fully equipped kitchen. Assisted by wife Lisa May and family members, Tom has expanded his 'business empire' to Callander with a bakery and fish shop adjoining his popular 'chippie'. He also runs a tearoom in the village of Balquhidder which is always busy - home baking of course! Situated in the heart of the Trossachs (Rob Roy country whose grave is at Balquhidder) with magnificent scenery all around you this is the perfect place base to stay and travel. Member of The Scotch Beef Club.

Open: *All year*	**Disabled:** *Dining only*
No. Rooms: *14 En suite 14*	**Swimming Pool/Health Club:** *No*
Room telephones: *Yes*	**Conference Facilities:** *No*
TV in Rooms: *Yes*	**Price Guide:** *Double £185.00 - £265.00 (suites)*
Pets: *No*	**Location:** *11 mls north of Callander on A84. Turn right at*
Children: *Yes*	*Kingshouse Hotel - 6 mls straight along Glen road.*

TOR-NA-COILLE HOTEL & RESTAURANT

Inchmarlo Road, Banchory, Royal Deeside. AB31 4AB

Tel: 01330 822242 Fax: 01330 824012

Email: info@tornacoille.com www.tornacoille.com

Stunning and elegant Victorian mansion (circa 1873) situated at the west end of Banchory. Surrounded by attractive wooded parkland and garden it has an imposing position on a raised level. I had my eye on this one when ownership changed in 2010 and Phillip J Fleming (known to me personally) was appointed General Manager. There has been a complete transformation at this hotel which has involved a lot of hard work and a sound financial investment. Complete overhaul of all bedrooms – I spent a night here and it's quite clear that the refurbishment has been planned with every comfort demanded by the modern day guest but retaining the features of a bygone era. Absolute luxury in the master bedrooms with superior furnishings and every amenity. The theme of high standards extends to the kitchen where award winning head chef Robert Ramsay displays all his culinary skills. Seasonal and fresh produce. Choice of a la carte, bistro/light meals and a very popular Sunday lunch. The main lounge area with open fire a cosy feature – great ambience and staff are very attentive and friendly. Elevator to all rooms. Weddings and corporate events welcome. Free WiFi. This is Royal Deeside Country – explore the castle & whisky trails or just climb a mountain! Or just enjoy the peace and contentment at Tor-Na-Coille.

Open: *All year*		**Swimming Pool/Health Club:** *No*	
No. Rooms: *25 En Suite 25*		**Conference Facilities:** *Yes*	
Room telephones: *Yes + WiFi*		**Price Guide:** *Single £70.00 - £85.00*	
TV in Rooms: *Yes*		*Double £105.00 - £160.00*	
Pets: *Arrangement*	**Children:** *Yes*	*Dinner a la carte*	
Disabled: *Yes*		**Location:** *West end of Banchory opposite golf club*	

SKIRLING HOUSE

Skirling, Biggar, Lanarkshire. ML12 6HD
Tel: 01899 860274   Fax: 01899 860255
Email: enquiry@skirlinghouse.com   www.skirlinghouse.com

This house, built in 1908, was designed by the famous architect Ramsay Traquair for Lord Carmichael as a country retreat. Skirling is a small attractive village just outside Biggar on the A72 to Peebles and the property is situated by the village green. The house has retained the original theme with carvings, rich fabrics, antiques and fine paintings - a feature is the 16th century Florentine carved ceiling which is much admired by guests. Bob and Isobel Hunter have made this an oasis of great comfort, quality cuisine and hospitality and there is a very informal but friendly and relaxing atmosphere. The award of 5 Gold Stars Guest House from VisitScotland is fully merited - bedrooms are tastefully decorated in keeping with the house and offer every comfort. The house menus (dinner is a set menu) change daily and make excellent use of fresh seasonal produce from the garden. Good selection and a sound quality of food with fine farmhouse cheeses. Meals are served in the conservatory with views over the magnificent lawn and gardens to the rear. A must for the more discerning visitor. A very skilled operation here and highly recommended. Only a short distance from Edinburgh.

Open: *March - December*	**Price Guide:** *Single £90.00 - £115.00 (inc. dinner)*
No. Rooms: *5 En Suite 5*	*B&B £60.00 - £85.00*
Room telephones: *Yes + WiFi*	*Double £160.00 - £180.00 (inc. dinner)*
TV in Rooms: *Yes*	*B&B £100.00 - £130.00*
Pets: *Yes* **Children:** *Yes*	**Location:** *2 mls from Biggar on A72 overlooking*
Disabled: *Yes*	*village green.*

Scottish
TOURIST BOARD
★★★★★
GUEST HOUSE
GOLD

THE HARBOUR INN & RESTAURANT

The Square, Bowmore, Isle of Islay. PA43 7JR
Tel: 01496 810330   Fax: 01496 810990
Email: info@harbour-inn.com   www.harbour-inn.com

An absolute paradise on this famous distillery Isle of Islay 'away from it all' - this hebridean island is an oasis of tranquillity with magnificent sea views. You can definitely bond with nature here and feel cut off from the rest of the world. Head for The Harbour Inn & Restaurant at Bowmore – extremely attractive harbour setting with white washed exterior and conservatory lounge which offers panoramic views over Loch Indaal. After a 9 year period owners Neil and Carol Scott have built up an enviable reputation on this island retreat. VisitScotland 4 star gold award 'Restaurant with Rooms' is a barometer of the high standards of food and accommodation at this small traditional yet very 'cosy' hotel. Spacious, well furnished bedrooms are extremely comfortable. Intimate bar area creates a wonderful ambience. The real 'foodie' will not be disappointed here. This is award winning food and demonstrates a highly skilled culinary operation. Sophiscated menus with seafood on your doorstep an obvious choice. 'The Inns Over-by', a short distance from the hotel offers 4 superb en suite bedrooms with its own conservatory. Breakfast is taken at the hotel. The adventure and anticipation begins with the ferry crossing from Kennacraig. Highly recommended.

Open: *All year*	**Swimming Pool/Health Club:** *No*
No. Rooms: *7 En Suite 7*	**Conference Facilities:** *No*
Room telephones: *Yes*	**Price Guide:** *Double £135.00 – £165.00*
TV in Rooms: *Yes*	**Location:** *Ferry from Kennacraig (just south of Tarbert,*
Pets: *No* **Children:** *Over 10*	*Loch Fyne) to Port Askaig or Port Ellen; follow*
Disabled: *Unsuitable*	*signs for Bowmore*

ROMAN CAMP COUNTRY HOUSE

Off Main Street, Callander, Perthshire. FK17 8BG
Tel: 01877 330003
Email: mail@romancamphotel.co.uk   www.romancamphotel.co.uk

This country house, just off the main street in Callander, (just be careful at the entrance) is set amongst wonderful woodland and garden and rippling river nearby. Quite a haven in itself. Originally built in 1625 for the Dukes of Perth as a hunting lodge it still retains that aura – roaring log fires to welcome you with extremely comfortable public rooms to enjoy that afternoon tea. Each of the 15 bedrooms have their own distinctive theme – spacious and comfortable with nice extra 'touches'. Apart from a great afternoon tea, head chef Ian McNaught, well-known for his culinary skills, provides meals using quality ingredients adding flair and imagination in keeping with an AA 3 rosette award. Well-placed to tour the Trossachs which is an area of outstanding beauty in Scotland. No doubt an ideal venue for weddings (on an exclusive basis is recommended). Staff always extremely professional and friendly. I have that 'feel good' factor when I stop here for a blether with resident proprietors Eric & Marion Brown who are renowned for their attention to detail and a warm welcome.

Open: *All year*	**Swimming Pool/Health Club:** *No*
No. Rooms: *15 En Suite 15*	**Conference Facilities:** *Up to 100*
Room telephones: *Yes*	**Price Guide:** *Single from £95.00 - £155.00*
TV in Rooms: *Yes* **Pets:** *Yes*	*Double from £155.00 - £230.00*
Children: *Yes*	**Location:** *East End of Callander. Main Street from*
Disabled: *Yes*	*Stirling turn left down drive for 300 yards.*

LOCH NESS LODGE HOTEL

Drumnadrochit, Inverness-shire. IV63 6TU
Tel: 01456 450342   Fax: 01456 450429
Email: info@lochness-hotel.com   www.lochness-hotel.com

Dating back to around 1740, this unusual hotel is synonymous with the famous Loch from which it takes its name. Once the home of a colonial tea planter, it stands in eight acres of delightful woodland grounds, now incorporating a pretty and exciting children's 'log house' and natural wooden play area, locally made. Situated 14 miles from Inverness on the Fort William road, and 1 mile from the famous Urquhart Castle, this is a favourite spot for tourists. Bedrooms are elegant and offer every comfort with the Glenurquhart suite a firm favourite - spacious with some nice personal touches. There are even some ground floor rooms for ease of access. The restaurant serves a fusion of modern and traditional cuisine: local venison, wild mushrooms and fresh garden vegetables. The hotel is linked to a Visitor Centre with its unique exhibition which attracts people from around the world. Log fires, friendly staff, unique bar specialising in Malt Whiskies, outstanding cuisine and first class service make a holiday at the Loch Ness Lodge Hotel a memorable experience. Corporate enquiries welcome. Your host: Gillian Skinner.

Open: *Closed mid Oct - mid March*	**Swimming Pool/Health Club:** *No*
No. Rooms: *50 En Suite 50*	**Conference Facilities:** *Max. 120*
Room telephones: *Yes + WiFi*	**Price Guide:** *Single from £65.00 p.p.p.n.*
TV in Rooms: *Yes*	*Double from £90.00 per room per night*
Pets: *No* **Children:** *Yes*	*(Ground floor rooms)*
Disabled: *Dining only*	**Location:** *14 miles south of Inverness on Fort William Road*

Scottish TOURIST BOARD
★★★
HOTEL

ULLINISH COUNTRY LODGE

Struan, Isle of Skye, Inverness-shire. IV56 8FD
Tel: 01470 572214   Fax: 01470 572341
Email: enquiries@ullinish-country-lodge.co.uk   www.ullinish-country-lodge.co.uk

If you want to 'get away from it all' Ullinish Country Lodge is the ideal place to just 'chill out' as they say now. Classified as a 'restaurant with rooms' this country lodge offers extremely high standards of hotel keeping. I have stayed here on 3 occasions – 4 of the bedrooms are quite spacious and luxurious and 2 are smaller but very snug and cosy. All the extra touches as you would expect from a 5 star establishment. I really like the lounge area with open fire where canapes are served before dinner. Great dinner menu and chef makes good use of local ingredients and there is an emphasis now on seafood which couldn't be more local. From loch & sea to the plate! AA 3 rosette restaurant – expectations are high for this award. AA breakfast award. Exact technique, balance and depth of flavour are important. There can be no doubt that Brian & Pamela Howard have taken this country lodge to a new level. A short distance from Dunvegan Castle (home of The MacLeods) other places to visit are Glenbrittle, Portnalong and Elgol in the south. Staffin & Uig in the north.

Open: *All year except Jan*
No. Rooms: *6 En Suite 6*
Room telephones: *No*
TV in Rooms: *Yes*
Pets: *No* **Children:** *Over 16*
Disabled: *Dining only*

Swimming Pool/Health Club: *No*
Conference Facilities: *No*
Price Guide: *Single from £90.00*
Double from £130.00
Location: *9 miles south of Dunvegan on Sligachan Road*

Scottish TOURIST BOARD
★★★★★
RESTAURANT WITH ROOMS
GOLD

AA ❀ ❀ ❀

THE SCOTCH BEEF CLUB

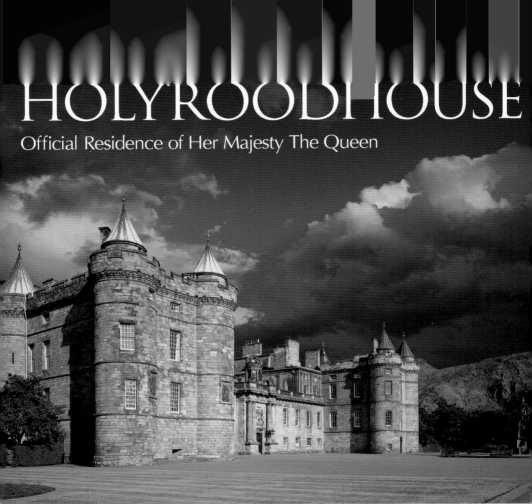

HOLYROODHOUSE

Official Residence of Her Majesty The Queen

Best known as the home of Mary, Queen of Scots, the Palace was the setting for many dramatic episodes in her short and turbulent reign.

A visit now includes a special display of the Order of the Thistle, the highest honour in Scotland.

Open daily, except during royal visits.

Enjoy a year's unlimited admission if you purchase your ticket directly from the Palace.

0131 556 5100 www.royalcollection.org.uk

THE ATHOLL

11, Atholl Crescent,Edinburgh. EH3 8HA
Tel: 08447 360047

Email: info@theatholl.com www.theatholl.com www.icmi.co.uk

This is Edinburgh's most exclusive hotel located in the New Town near the West End of the City. Georgian building but the interior has been transformed in a contemporary classical design. Personally, I have never viewed such a property with so much awe. There are 4 amazing suites. The 3 bedroomed Abercromby & Dundonald Suites, the 2 bedroomed Cluny Suite & the 1 bedroom Palmerston Suite. The suites are opulent with bespoke furnishings and wine and cheese in custom-made chiller cabinets. No expense spared here – cuisine with your own in-house chef trained by the renowned Albert Roux OBE, KFO who is head of the famous cooking dynasty behind such establishments as Le Gavroche which was the first ever restaurant in the UK to be awarded three Michelin Stars. Butler service (24 hours) and terraced suite complete with barbeque at the rear of the property. This is luxury personified and a 'home away from home' with all the modern amenities one would expect. Certainly suit business and leisure visitors – only minutes from Princes Street, The Castle, the railway station and 20 minutes from the airport. This can only be described as pure indulgement.

Open: *All year*	**Swimming Pool/Health Club:** *No*
No. Suites: *4*	**Conference Facilities:** *Boardroom up to 20*
Room telephones: *Yes*	**Price Guide:** *£1,000.00 - £2,500.00 per night*
TV in Suites: *All rooms within suites have this facility. Plus all other up-to-date technology for business/social needs.*	**Location:** *West end of Edinburgh near Shandwick Place on the main A8 coming in from the airport.*

CHAMPAGNE
BILLECART-SALMON
Maison Fondée en 1818

www.champagne-billecart.fr

GREYWALLS & CHEZ ROUX

Muirfield, Gullane, East Lothian. EH31 2EG
Tel: 01620 842144   Fax: 01620 842241
Email: enquiries@greywalls.co.uk   www.greywalls.co.uk   www.icmi.co.uk

This is a magnificent country house designed by Sir Edwin Lutyens just 17 miles from Edinburgh. Now a member of the prestigious Relais & Chateaux it overlooks the famous open championship golf course which returns to Muirfield in 2013. The gardens alone are worth a visit. Now operated by Inverlochy Castle Management International, Greywalls has become one of the premier hotels in Scotland which will rival any other - the food operation under the direction of the renowned Albert Roux OBE, KFO who is head of the famous cooking dynasty behind such establishments as Le Gavroche which was the first ever restaurant in the UK to be awarded three Michelin Stars is a culinary paradise. Head chef Derek Johnstone is already making a name for himself and I have sampled the fayre myself. French influence obvious and the choice of pike quenelle a pure delight. When I stayed here the bedrooms offered every comfort – spacious and well furnished with excellent en suite facilities. The influence of Inverlochy Castle where I stay for 2 days every year certainly prevails. This influence permutates throughout – service and attention to detail could not be faulted. An option here is the Colonel's house which sleeps 8 and offers more privacy. Plenty to do and see in East Lothian including golf! Your host and General Manager: Duncan Fraser. Highly recommended.

Open: *All year*	**Conference Facilities:** *Yes*
No. Rooms: 23	**Price Guide:** *Single £210.00 - £300.00*
Room telephones: *Yes*	*Double £230.00 - £320.00*
TV in Rooms: *Yes*	*Caddy's Closet (single) £80.00 - £105.00*
Pets: *By request* **Children:** *Yes*	**Location:** *Last turning left after leaving Gullane*
Swimming Pool/Health Club: *No*	*travelling East (N. Berwick).*

ICMI
The Collection

ICMI was founded by the senior management of Inverlochy Castle Hotel, Scotland's most renowned small luxury hotel, to provide a consulting and management service to the hotel and hospitality industries.

The management team has the expertise, experience and structure to assist small to medium size businesses to acheive profitability through sound management and robust innovative marketing. ICMI won Hotel Management Company of the Year in 2010, 2011 and 2012.

Inverlochy Castle
Highlands
www.inverlochycastlehotel.com
Tel: +44 (0)1397 702177
Email: info@inverlochy.co.uk

The Atholl
Edinburgh
www.theatholl.com
Tel: +44 (0)8447 360047
Email: info@theatholl.com

Greywalls & Chez Roux
near Edinburgh
www.greywalls.co.uk
Tel: +44 (0)1620 842144
Email: enquiries@greywalls.co.uk

Inver Lodge & Chez Roux
Highlands
www.inverlodge.com
Tel: +44 (0)1571 844496
Email: stay@inverlodge.com

Alladale Wilderness Reserve
Highlands
www.alladale.co.uk
Tel: +44 (0)1463 716416
Email: enquiries@alladale.co.uk

Rocpool Reserve & Chez Roux
Inverness
www.rocpool.com
Tel: +44 (0)1463 240089
Email: info@rocpool.com

Blanefield House
near Turnberry
www.blanefieldhouse.com
Tel: +44 (0)1397 702177
Email: info@blanefieldhouse.com

Rocpool Reserve Apartments
Edinburgh
www.rocpool.com
Tel: +44 (0)1620 842144
Email: apartments@rocpool.com

ICMI manages a number of hotels and exclusive use private houses, all united by a passion for the finest cuisine, service and levels of comfort and discretion.

Email: norbertlieder@icmi.co.uk   Tel: +44 (0)01397 702177   www.icmi.co.uk

Registered office: Torlundy, Fort William PH33 6SN Tel: 01397 702177 Fax: 01397 702953

INVERLOCHY CASTLE

Torlundy, Fort William. PH33 6SN

Tel: 01397 702177 Fax: 01397 702953   USA Toll Free Tel: 1-888 424 0106

Email: info@inverlochy.co.uk www.inverlochycastlehotel.com www.icmi.co.uk

A member of the prestigious Relais & Chateaux this is an outstanding castle property set in magnificent landscaped gardens just north of Fort William. It nestles below Ben Nevis in a stunning highland setting. This was my 17th stay at Inverlochy Castle and once again it was the complete experience offering every comfort and quality of service. Without doubt it retains and maintains the finest traditions of hotel keeping. Bedrooms are spacious (especially the 3 main suites) with quality furnishings and décor in keeping with the traditional castle building. Combined with large en suite facilities the accommodation can only be described as luxurious. The talents of head chef Phil Carnegie are obvious – high technical skills with flair and imagination. A culinary triumph perfectly executed. **Michelin Star** award. In 1873 Queen Victoria described Inverlochy as the most lovely and romantic spot she had seen. I can only agree. The management team under the direction of Jane Watson, who has been here for 32 years, are to be congratulated. A warm welcome, peace and seclusion, with cuisine and wine cellar of the highest order and excellent service. Activities in the area include one of the busiest ski resorts in Scotland. Managed by Inverlochy Castle Management International.

Open: *All year.*	**Swimming Pool/Health Club:** *No*
No. Rooms: *18*	**Conference Facilities:** *Yes*
Room telephones: *Yes*	**Price Guide:** *Single £265-£375; Double/Twin £320-£550;*
TV in Rooms: *Yes*	*Suite £480-£695.*
Pets: *Yes* **Children:** *Yes*	**Location:** *3 miles north of Fort William. In the village*
Disabled: *Dining only*	*of Torlundy on A82.*

GOLD

★★★★★

RAMNEE HOTEL

Victoria Road, Forres, Moray. IV36 3BN
Tel: 01309 672410 Fax: 01309 673392
Email: info@ramneehotel.com   www.ramneehotel.com

This fine Edwardian mansion built in 1907 is situated in landscaped gardens to the east of the Royal Burgh of Forres. The Ramnee enjoys a certain amount of isolation but is in easy reach of the town centre which is famous for its parkland floral displays and architectural qualities. Over many years the Ramnee has enjoyed a reputation for consistently high standards of hotel keeping. The bedrooms are a delight, (with 4 poster if required) - elegant, and very comfortable, all with en suite facilities - many have views over the Moray Firth. The cuisine offered at lunch and evening is very traditional and features dishes prepared from the very best of Scotland's larder; guests can choose the informality of the bar or reserve a table in Hamblins Restaurant. There is a friendly atmosphere which radiates throughout the hotel. Golfing is high on the list of sporting activities in this area and businessmen make good use of the conference/seminar facilities, whilst the hotel is also now offering luxury, serviced bungalows in and around Forres. Also see entry for Inverness City Suites. Your host: Garry Dinnes.

Open: *All year.*	**Disabled**: *Dinner only*
No. Rooms: *18 En Suite 18*	**Swimming Pool/Health Club:** *No*
Room telephones: *Yes + WiFi*	**Conference Facilities:** *Theatre up to 100*
TV in Rooms: *Yes*	**Price Guide:** *Single £90.00 - £150.00 Double £100.00 - £170.00*
Pets: *Yes*	**Location:** *A96 Aberdeen-Inverness off by-pass at roundabout*
Children: *Yes*	*to east of Forres - 500 yards on right*

GLENGARRY CASTLE HOTEL

Invergarry, Inverness-shire. PH35 4HW
Tel: 01809 501254 Fax: 01809 501207
Email: castle@glengarry.net   www.glengarry.net

Glengarry Castle commands a stunning position overlooking Loch Oich between Loch Ness and Loch Lochy in this popular area of Scotland. The ruins of Invergarry Castle, the ancient seat of the McDonnells of Glengarry - which gave shelter to Bonnie Prince Charlie before and after the battle of Culloden stands within sight of the hotel. A real family castle hotel the MacCallum family have been here since 1958 and are rightly proud of their achievements - so many enjoyable visits/overnight stays over a number of years. This Victorian building with grand entrance hall has all the ingredients of that bygone era with large reception and public room areas all with views to the garden and loch. The 26 bedrooms have all the ensuite comforts one would expect, some with four posters. True highland hospitality here with fresh produce being the key to successful traditional cooking - the old fashioned afternoon teas a daily highlight. There are a number of activities to enjoy including walks through extensive woodlands, boating on the loch, fishing and making use of the newly surfaced Elastosol tennis court. Perfect stop over for those travelling to Skye or Inverness and beyond. Your host - Donald MacCallum.

Open: *Mar. 22nd - Nov. 4th*	**Swimming Pool/Health Club:** *No*
No. Rooms: *26 En Suite 25*	**Conference Facilities:** *No*
Room telephones: *Yes*	**Price Guide:** *Single £70.00 - £80.00*
TV in Rooms: *Yes*	*Double £104.00 - £186.00*
Pets: *Yes* **Children:** *Yes*	**Location:** *One mile south of Invergarry on A82*
Disabled: *Limited*	*overlooking Loch Oich.*

AA ✿

INVERNESS CITY SUITES

2-7 High Street, Inverness. IV1 1HY
Tel: 01463 715218
Email: stay@invernesscitysuites.co.uk www.invernesscitysuites.co.uk

Ideally located in the middle of this grand highland city it is a short distance from the River Ness, the castle and the train/bus station. The apartments just exude quality – extremely spacious with bespoke furnishings and all modern amenities one would expect from a 4 star VisitScotland establishment. Lounge, dining and kitchen areas are quite amazing; the master bedrooms are en suite and the second bedroom has it's own bath or shower room. No expense spared here and obviously carefully planned with the comfort of the guest paramount. All apartments have been enhanced with a modern décor and a professional input expressing peace and tranquillity. With improvised planning an apartment can accommodate up to 6 people. Families very welcome. No need for housekeeping duties here – it's all done for you. And if you don't wish to eat 'at home' Inverness is noted for its culinary outlets. All within walking distance. This is a definite 'alternative' type of accommodation which offers all the comforts in a more relaxed (and private) atmosphere and where you can set your own timetable to suit your own requirements. Your contact here is Garry Dinnes who also operates the Ramnee Hotel in Forres (see separate entry).

Open: *All year.*		**Children:** *Yes*	**Disabled**: *Unsuitable*
No. Rooms: *11 (6 apartments)*		**Swimming Pool/Health Club:** *Treatments can be arranged*	
En suite: *Yes*		**Conference Facilities:** *No*	
Room telephones: *Yes*		**Price Guide:** *1 bedroom apartment £90.00 - £160.00 (seasonal)*	
TV in Rooms: *Yes*		*2 bedroom apartment £160.00 - £270.00 (seasonal)*	
Pets: *By arrangement*		**Location:** *High Street opp. Inverness Town House*	

CULLODEN HOUSE HOTEL

Culloden, Inverness. IV2 7BZ
Tel: 01463 790461   Fax: 01463 792181
Email: info@cullodenhouse.co.uk   www.cullodenhouse.co.uk

Quite a majestic entrance to this property – a very stately mansion with all the 'trappings' of Bonnie Prince Charlie and the last battle on British soil in April 1746. The sweeping manicured lawns and building-clad virginia creeper cannot fail to impress the visitor and rightly so – the current 'Bonnie Prince Charlie' has been a visitor here of course. Within the elegance and charm of this hotel is true Highland hospitality – guests are met with a genuine welcome – there is a very friendly and relaxed atmosphere which immediately puts you at ease. The 'hands on' approach from General Manager Stephen Davies is quite evident - he seems to be everywhere at the one time! Talented and devoted head chef Michael Simpson (26 years) is known by reputation for his culinary skills and holds the 2 AA red rosette award. Also, Eat Scotland Silver Award. Bedrooms and ensuite are lavish in their size (rooms 15 and 16 are my favourites) with quality furnishings and every modern amenity. Public areas form the same theme - complete comfort in a quite regal style. The complete experience. The City of Inverness has itself a lot to offer the visitor – there are also a number of visitor and historical attractions in the area. Airport 15 minutes. Highly recommended.

Open: *All year*	**Swimming Pool/Health Club:** *No*
No. Rooms: *28 En Suite 28*	**Conference Facilities:** *Up to 40*
Room telephones: *Yes*	**Price Guide:** *Single £175.00 - £365.00*
TV in Rooms: *Yes*	*Double £250.00 - £395.00 (suite)*
Pets: *Yes* **Children:** *Yes*	*Enquire about seasonal breaks*
Disabled: *Not suitable*	**Location:** *3mls from Inverness & 3mls from airport*

THE KINGSMILLS HOTEL (INC. THE KINGSCLUB & SPA)

Culcabock Road, Inverness. IV2 3LP
Tel: 01463 257100   Fax: 01463 712984
Email: reservations@kingsmillshotel.com   www.kingsmillshotel.com

An extremely popular destination, The Kingsmills is synonomous with the City of Inverness. Perfectly placed on the periphery of the city with ample car parking. The new Kingsclub & Spa has been a great 'success story' and offers every modern comfort. Bedrooms (37) are of luxurious proportions, are air-conditioned and have wonderful views over the golf course. The main hotel is directly opposite where this year I stayed 4 nights. There are 77 bedrooms within the main building but from the moment you arrive you will experience a very personal touch. Reception staff proved to be very efficient (and friendly - 'well kent' face Bill Sloan on concierge, a tonic for all). Great ambience prevails throughout this hotel. A very skilled food & beverage operation and once again I enjoyed my dinner in the conservatory dining area. Guests have the full use of the swimming pool within the main hotel. Corporate events are important with a professional dedicated team to take care of everything. I attend a private dinner party here every September for a group of 20 and it goes 'without a hitch'. Fond memories indeed stretching back to 1977 when it only had 21 bedrooms. Favourite room number 200. Lift to all floors. Host & General Manager: Craig Ewan.

Open: *All year*	**Disabled:** *Yes (Excellent)*
No. Rooms: *114*	**Swimming Pool/Health Club:** *Yes*
Room telephones: *Yes*	**Conference Facilities:** *Yes - 3 venues for up to 80*
TV in Rooms: *Yes*	**Price Guide:** *Room rate: £90.00 - £275.00 (suite)*
Pets: *By arrangement*	**Location:** *Culcabock Road next to Inverness Golf course.*
Children: *Yes*	*1 mile from city centre.*

ROCPOOL RESERVE & CHEZ ROUX

Culduthel Road, Inverness. IV2 4AG
Tel: 01463 240089   Fax: 01463 248431
Email: info@rocpool.com   www.rocpool.com   www.icmi.co.uk

Unique 'boutique' hotel snugly situated within a leafy suburb of Inverness. It is quite exceptional. "Think of everything you know about hotels then forget it all instantly – Rocpool will redefine the experience for ever," are the opening words on the hotel brochure and having personally sampled the Rocpool experience I couldn't agree more. Luxurious bedrooms (some with hot tub) and bespoke soft furnishings are obvious. The theme throughout this hotel is all about quality whether it's the cuisine, accommodation, service or housekeeping. Known by reputation, Albert Roux OBE, KFO is head of the famous cooking dynasty behind such establishments as Le Gavroche which was the first ever restaurant in the UK to be awarded three Michelin Stars. I have dined here on quite a few occasions - there is a mixture of French and Scottish dishes (including signature dish Pike Quenelle) and diners expectations are fully met. Balance and depth of flavour using quality ingredients allied with the talents of the kitchen brigade and you have the perfect dining experience. For those wishing to compromise on time but not taste try the 4 course Rouxpress at £14.95! This is a very professional operation driven by General Manager Niki Gillies and her team. VisitScotland 5 stars and part of Inverlochy Castle Management International. Highly recommended.

Open: *All year*	**Swimming Pool/Health Club:** *No*	
No. Rooms: *11*	**Conference Facilities:** *Yes*	
Room telephones: *Yes*	**Price Guide:** *Single £150.00 - £175.00*	
TV in Rooms: *Yes*	*Double £185.00 - £395.00*	
Pets: *No* **Children:** *Yes*	**Location:** *Make for Inverness Castle and proceed up*	
Disabled: *Yes*	*Castle Street to Culduthel Road.*	

THE STEADINGS AT THE GROUSE & TROUT

Flichity, Farr, Inverness-shire. IV2 6XD
Tel: 01808 521314   Fax: 01808 521741
Email: stay@steadingshotel.co.uk   www.steadingshotel.co.uk

This is a real 'wee gem'. Travel down Strathnairn for 8 miles on the Fort Augustus road (B851) clearly marked from the main A9 just south of Inverness. Another most enjoyable overnight stay in the company of the resident proprietors Mary and David Allen. Formerly a farm steading circa 1860 it is now an extremely well restored and refurbished property. Care has been taken with the 8 en suite bedrooms – all refurbished to a high standard with extra touches. 2 bedroom 'cottages' attached to the hotel itself offer a slightly different option with access to the garden or the gazebo if you want a smoke! Gardens and surrounds are immaculate and the large conservatory looking out over the hills instills a sense of peace and contentment. Good wholesome cooking here (generous portions I should add) and a real cracking prawn cocktail not seen on many menus these days. Service first class and a real friendly ambience prevails throughout. Game shooting/loch/river/sea fishing available locally. David & Mary extend a real warm welcome to all their guests and its really a 'home from home' atmosphere. Culloden battlefield just up the road – plenty to do and see or just take a wee stroll in the evening. Really good value for money. Favourite room 'Flichity' which is one of the 'cottage bedrooms'.

Open: *March - October*	**Swimming Pool/Health Club:** *No*
No. Rooms: *8 En Suite*	**Conference Facilities:** *Up to 10*
Room telephones: *Yes* **TV in Rooms:** *Yes*	**Price Guide:** *Single £82.00*
Pets: *Yes (by arrangement)*	*Double from £99.00 - £165.00*
Children: *Yes (by arrangement)*	**Location:** *Strathnairn between Farr & Croachy. 5mls*
Disabled: *Yes (dining only)*	*sth of Inverness take B851 to Ft. Augustus.*

ALLERTON HOUSE

Oxnam Road, Jedburgh. TD8 6QQ
Tel: 01835 869633   Fax: 01835 869941

Email: info@allertonhouse.co.uk   www.allertonhouse.co.uk

A real 'home from home' would be the best way of describing Allerton House. A very successful operation with a warm welcome from your hosts Christopher and Carol Longden - well known within the hospitality trade. Indeed, well known for their dedication with the comfort of the guest paramount. A stately mansion house with very attractive gardens it commands an elevated position overlooking the Royal Burgh of Jedburgh. There are 6 elegant en suite bedrooms ranging from The Abbey Room on the ground floor (disabled access) to the spacious Queen Mary Suite with 4 poster and views of the garden. Double/twin and single optional. Superior furnishings, linen & drapes extol the virtues of each room. Every modern amenity includes digital TV, ipod docking station, mini bar, hospitality tray and many extras. The Macallan lounge with roaring fire offers every comfort – the breakfast is a meal in itself and will last you all day. There are a number of good eating places within the town and your hosts will advise. Very popular with 'walkers & ramblers' but an opportunity for all who visit the borders of Scotland and also enjoy excellent accommodation at a reasonable cost. A host of countryside pursuits to hand and places of historical interest to visit. Great ambience at Allerton House and a genuine, warm and friendly atmosphere prevails throughout.

Open: *All year*	**Swimming Pool/Health Club:** *Within 5 mins. walk*
No. Rooms: *6 En Suite 6*	**Conference Facilities:** *No*
Room telephones: *No*	**Price Guide:** *Single £55.00 - £70.00*
TV in Rooms: *Yes*	*Double/Twin £80.00 - £95.00*
Pets: *No* **Children:** *Yes*	**Location:** *Edinburgh 50 mls. Turn off A68 opp. Jedburgh*
Disabled: *Yes*	*Abbey into Oxnam Road - 500 yds. on right.*

For the last 50 years, MORTIMER'S OF GRANTOWN ON SPEY has supplied the best in fishing and outdoor leisure equipment to discerning sports men and women from all over the world.

We stock every conceivable quality accessory including the full range of Hardy fishing tackle and a vast range of equipment from other manufacturers. Most of the leading makes of outdoor clothing for men and women are stocked together with a full range of shooting accessories and ammunition. We even have our own Mortimer's range of single malt and blended whisky. Of course, supplying equipment is only part of our service to you. We are also able to supply fishing permits, from the Strathspey Angling Association, for both banks of a nearby 6 mile stretch of the River Spey. Tuition can be arranged with our experienced ghillies and with the use of the best tackle - hired from us!

We look forward to meeting you.

MORTIMER'S,
3 HIGH STREET,
GRANTOWN ON SPEY,
MORAY, PH26 3HB.
TEL: 01479 872684.
e-mail: mortimers@spey.fsnet.co.uk
www.mortimersofspeyside.co.uk

BALLATHIE HOUSE

Kinclaven, By Stanley, Perthshire. PH1 4QN
Tel: 01250 883268   Fax: 01250 883396
Email address: email@ballathiehousehotel.com   www.ballathiehousehotel.com

This is a magnificent property situated in its own country estate overlooking the River Tay noted for its fishing. The main driveway and garden policies in a woodland setting are immaculate. This house of character dates back to 1850 and is only a short drive from Perth. The main house is simply stunning – bedrooms and public areas all retain that elegance associated with a country house and offer every comfort. An option is the very sensitive development of the riverside rooms and suites with a short walk to the main building. Exceptional views over the Tay. A further option is the Sportsman's lodge rooms (en suite) and one self catering apartment. Sophisticated food and beverage operation here - the technical skills and an ambition to achieve high standards are obvious. The dedication and passion of award winning head chef Scott Scorer is clearly evident in the daily changing menu where he makes the best use of Scottish produce. You will not be disappointed. Ideal venue for weddings. Service and housekeeping could not be faulted. A lot of repeat business here which means once you have visited Ballathie House you will return. Highly recommended.

Open: *All year*	**Swimming Pool/Health Club:** *No*
No. Rooms: *53 En Suite 53*	**Conference Facilities:** *Boardroom meetings to 30*
Room telephones: *Yes*	**Price Guide:** *Single from £60.00 B&B; Double or Twin from*
TV in Rooms: *Yes*	*£100.00 B&B - Special seasonal midweek breaks*
Pets: *Yes* **Children:** *Yes*	**Location:** *Off A9, 2 miles North of Perth through Stanley,*
Disabled: *Yes*	*or off A93 at Beech hedge and signs.*

LYNNFIELD HOTEL & RESTAURANT

Holm Road, St. Ola, Kirkwall. KW15 1SU
Tel: 01856 872505
Email: office@lynnfield.co.uk www.lynnfieldhotel.com

A great success story this is now one of the premier destinations on the islands of Orkney. Well known by reputation Malcolm Stout and partner Lorna Reid (who moved from Westray in 2006) have managed, through a lot of hard work, to transform Lynnfield to a luxury VisitScotland 4 star property. Ideal location on the periphery of Kirkwall and next to the Highland Park Distillery. 10 very luxurious bedrooms (including 1 disabled, 3 suites & 2 four posters) – offer every comfort. Their reputation for excellent Orcadian cuisine has followed from Westray, with daily evolving menus. Terrific view over the bay from the restaurant sets the tone for a wonderful dining experience. It's difficult sometimes for me to find a place of this quality on the islands of Scotland – on my visits to Orkney I always found there was plenty to do and see – 3 days to cover visits to Skara Brae, the Ortak factory, the distillery and a wee drive over The Churchill Barriers or take an evening stroll into the town and do a bit of window shopping. Make sure this one is on your itinerary when planning your trip to Orkney. You will not be disappointed. Well recommended.

Open: *All year*	**Swimming Pool/Health Club:** *No*
No. Rooms: *10 En Suite 10*	**Conference Facilities:** *Up to 30*
Room telephones: *Yes*	**Price Guide:** *Single occupancy £85.00*
TV in Rooms: *Yes* **Pets:** *Arrangement*	*Double £110.00 - £150.00 (3 suites)*
Children: *Over 12*	**Location:** *A961 Holm Road where indicated.*
Disabled: *1 room*	*Near Highland Park Distillery*

Scottish
TOURIST BOARD
★★★★
SMALL
HOTEL

INVER LODGE HOTEL & CHEZ ROUX

Lochinver, Sutherland. IV27 4LU
Tel: 01571 844496   Fax: 01571 844395
Email: stay@inverlodge.com   www.inverlodge.com   www.icmi.co.uk

My assessment last year was 'spot on' and this property now boasts a 5 star rating from VisitScotland. The final part of the refurbishment is now complete with the upgrade of the en suite facilities. Luxurious drapes, carpets and furniture throughout. The new bespoke Iolaire suite introduced 2 years ago is quite magnificent with own fireplace but all bedrooms/suites are extremely spacious and comfortable and all have panoramic views over the harbour and beyond. The cuisine (Chez Roux) has taken on a slightly French influence introduced by Albert Roux OBE, KFO who is head of the famous cooking dynasty behind such establishments as Le Gavroche which was the first ever restaurant in the UK to be awarded three Michelin Stars. The abundance of local fresh ingredients, especially fish from the harbour and wild chanterelles, are used in more traditional dishes. The view from the dining room is 'out of this world'. General Manager Nicholas Gorton maintains a high level of hospitality and he and his team deserve all the plaudits on their 5 star achievement. Guests return year on year. Service and housekeeping faultless. Plenty to do and see and once you have visited you will return. Great ambience and comes highly recommended. Managed by Inverlochy Castle Management International.

Open: *Early April-end Oct.*	**Swimming Pool/Health Club:** *No*
No. Rooms: *21*	**Conference Facilities:** *No*
Room telephones: *Yes*	**Price Guide:** *Single £115.00 - £150.00*
TV in Rooms: *Yes*	*Double £215.00 - £480.00*
Pets: *Yes* **Children:** *Yes*	**Location:** *Through village on A835 and turn left after*
Disabled: *Ground floor*	*village hall.*

THE FOUR SEASONS HOTEL
St. Fillans, Perthshire. PH6 2NF
Tel: 01764 685333 Fax: 01764 685444
Email:info@thefourseasonshotel.co.uk www.thefourseasonshotel.co.uk

The position of this hotel is quite stunning with panoramic views down Loch Earn and situated in the picturesque village of St. Fillans in Perthshire. Surrounded by hills and woodland it is one of the finest lochside locations in Scotland. Hands on approach from seasoned hotelier Andrew Low and his staff ensure a wonderful all round experience with the comfort of the guest paramount. A very robust food operation and the dedication of the kitchen brigade is obvious. Holder of the prestigous 2 AA rosette award for many years, there is a clear ambition to achieve high standards. During my overnight visits here I have sampled the fayre from the more formal Meall Reamhar restaurant and the bistro menu in the Tarken room. A wonderful dining experience on all occasions with views directly down the loch. Bedrooms offer every comfort with generous space and en suite facilities. Other options include 6 chalets or a self contained apartment which would suit a family. Cosy bar area and from his many adventures Andrew has introduced an oriental theme which mellows in with the more traditional décor. Corporate enquiries welcome. Event weekends are popular (wine tasting and painting etc). Also enquire about seasonal breaks. I like The Four Seasons – great ambience and 'laid back' culture. Include this one on your annual itinerary – you will not be disappointed. Recommended for all the right reasons.

Open: *March - December inclusive*
No. Rooms: *12 En Suite 12; 6 chalets*
Room telephones: *Yes*
TV in Rooms: *Yes*
Pets: *Yes* **Children:** *Yes*
Disabled: *No*

Swimming Pool/Health Club: *No*
Conference Facilities: *Up to 36*
Price Guide: *Single £54.00 B&B chalet to £141.00 DB&B 4 poster*
Double from £61.00 B&B to £116.00 DB&B
Chalets £54 B&B to £87 DB&B. All pppn
Location: *A85 - west end of St. Fillans village.*

KIRROUGHTREE HOUSE

Newton Stewart, Wigtownshire DG8 6AN
Tel: 01671 402141   Fax: 01671 402425
Email: info@kirroughtreehouse.co.uk   www.kirroughtreehouse.co.uk

No doubt one of my favourites in the south west of Scotland with a great core of loyal customers who return year after year. The drive up to the hotel encompasses 8 acres of landscaped gardens which are magnificent, more so when the 'rhodies' are in bloom. This unusual building has been carefully restored and refurbished in keeping with the original house with varying degrees of comfort – from standard, de luxe and the opulent regal suite. All are elegant in their own right – my own room (downstairs) with entrance/exit from the rear and lift to ground floor, was massive. The ensuite facility was as large as a bedroom! The elegant theme continues through to the wood-panelled, extremely comfortable lounge (where you order dinner) and the 2 dining rooms. Matthew McWhir, head chef, produces a first class dining experience – so consistent over the years he works miracles in the kitchen. Menus short but creative – obviously good prep work here. Great ambience throughout. Service very professional and friendly. Good base for exploring the delights of the south west. Your host: 'well kent' Jim Stirling.

Open: *Feb 14-Jan 3*	**Swimming Pool/Health Club:** *No*
No. Rooms: *17 En Suite 17*	**Conference Facilities:** *Max 20*
Room telephones: *Yes*	**Price Guide:** *Single £115.00-£120.00 Double £190.00-£270.00*
TV in Rooms: *Yes*	*Reduced rates for extended breaks*
Pets: *By arrangement* **Children:** *Over 10* **Location:**	*From A75 take A712 New Galloway Road.*
Disabled: *Limited*	*Hotel 300 yards on left.*

THE MANOR HOUSE

Gallanach Road, Oban, Argyll. PA34 4LS
Tel: 01631 562087   Fax: 01631 563053
Email: info@manorhouseoban.com   www.manorhouseoban.com

On the outskirts of Oban just beyond the ferry terminal this Georgian House, built in 1780 commands an enviable position overlooking the Oban bay to the islands beyond. Known to me for many years it is situated in a quiet spot away from the main centre of Oban and retains the charm and elegance of a bygone era. Under the personal supervision of General Manager Gregor MacKinnon, this small hotel offers every comfort one would expect from a VisitScotland 4 star rating and cuisine to match. Bedrooms are extremely comfortable (some with views over the bay), public rooms are spacious, well furnished and cosy with log fire in the winter (when I stayed). The talents of head chef Sean Squire and his kitchen brigade are obvious and over the years this has proved to be a wonderful dining experience. Fresh fish (as one would expect) lamb and game in season could be your choice. Ideal stay for a day journey to the island of Mull or explore the beautiful Argyll coastland north or south of Oban. Breath-taking views from many points along the way. Always an enjoyable stay over a number of years and still a firm favourite. Ideally placed for boarding The Hebridean Princess.

Open: *All year except Christmas*	**Swimming Pool/Health Club:** *No*
No. Rooms: *11 En Suite 11*	**Conference Facilities:** *No*
Room telephones: *Yes*	**Price Guide:** *Single £140.00 – £250.00 (includes dinner)*
TV in Rooms: *Yes*	*Double £185.00 – £285.00 (includes dinner)*
Pets: *By request* **Children:** *Over 12*	*Enquire about seasonal breaks.*
Disabled: *Restricted*	**Location:** *200yds past ferry terminal on Gallanach Road.*

AA

HEBRIDEAN PRINCESS

Kintail House, Skipton, N. Yorks. BD23 2DE
Tel: 01756 704704   Fax: 01756 704794
Email: reservations@hebridean.co.uk   www.hebridean.co.uk

Sailing mainly from Oban and Greenock, experience the most beautiful scenery of the British Isles aboard the luxurious Hebridean Princess. This small and unique cruise ship, chartered twice by Queen Elizabeth has immaculately maintained teak decks and polished brass. She cruises Scotland's west coast, Western and Northern Isles in inimitable style. The epitome of understated elegance, from the panoramic Tiree Lounge to the plush Columba Restaurant, the public rooms and 30 spacious cabins are beautifully furnished throughout. Imaginative menus are created using the freshest local produce to bring you memorable breakfasts and elegant dining, with first class service from one of the best crews afloat. Hebridean Princess sails from March until November with a maximum of 50 guests. 2013 marks her 25th season of cruising and over the years she has explored some of Scotland's most remote regions, sailing west as far as St Kilda, and north to the Orkneys, Shetlands as well as visiting Norway, Ireland, France, the Channel Isles and England's south coast. Hebridean Princess offers fully inclusive cruises of between 4 and 10 nights including all meals, alcoholic and non alcoholic drinks, shore excursions and gratuities.

Open: *From March to November*
No. Cabins: *30 En Suite 30*
TV in Rooms: *Yes*
Pets: *No*
Children: *Aged 9 and over*
Disabled: *Unsuitable*

Swimming Pool/Health Club: *No*
Conference Facilities: *No*
Price Guide: *7 nights fully inclusive from*
£1,930.00 – £9,950.00 per person
Location: *Argyll*

THE PARKLANDS HOTEL (& RESTAURANTS)

2 St. Leonard's Bank, Perth. PH2 8EB
Tel: 01738 622451

Email: info@theparklandshotel.com www.theparklandshotel.com

This hotel has won a plethora of awards – for the hotel itself and also the restaurant operation. Watched with great interest the progress made at this small town house, perfectly situated on the periphery of Perth, overlooking the South Inch. This Victorian mansion house has retained all its classical lines enhanced by very attractive gardens. Owners Scott and Penny Edwards have re-invested year on year and this hotel now ranks as the top pick in the City of Perth. Superior Bedrooms are spacious with excellent en suite facilities and jacuzzi in one of the bedrooms. Flat screen plasma TVs, DVDs, ipod docking and wireless broadband in every room. The public areas are very stylish and comfort of the guest paramount. The food produced here by the team, led by Graeme Pallister is exceptional – seasonal, well prepared dishes, using the rich natural larder that Perthshire offers. There is a quiet efficiency here with first rate service and attention to detail. The hotel is food focused with private dining, small wedding and corporate events all catered for. Small wedding enquiries welcome. A very relaxed and friendly atmosphere prevails throughout, making the hotel an ideal base for touring Perthshire and beyond. Only 45 minutes from Glasgow or Edinburgh. (Also see food entry under 63, Tay Street within the Good Food Book). Just go – you will not be disappointed. Ample car parking.

Open: *All year*	**Swimming Pool/Health Club:** *No*
No. Rooms: *15 En Suite 15*	**Conference Facilities:** *Up to 24*
Room telephones: *Yes + Wifi*	**Price Guide:** *Double £102.50 - £155.00*
TV in Rooms: *Flat screen plasma*	*Single £92.00 - £129.00 (enquire about seasonal breaks)*
Disabled: *Ground floor rooms/Dining*	**Location:** *From A90 head towards railway station.*
Pets: *Yes* **Children:** *Yes*	*Parklands on left at end of South Inch*

POOL HOUSE
Poolewe, By Achnasheen, Wester Ross. IV22 2LD
Tel: 01445 781272 Fax: 01445 781403
Email: stay@pool-house.co.uk www.pool-house.co.uk

This must be one of the finest locations in the highlands - stunning property on the shores of Loch Ewe. The panoramic views are exceptional and only a short walk from the famous Inverewe Gardens. A romantic haven indeed. Small, intimate and very exclusive, the Harrison family go to extreme lengths to make your stay one to remember - the bedrooms just exude opulence with quality furnishings and nice touches. Open decking with hot tub an option. New addition this year is the spectacular Potager 'cottage type' unit built within the gounds of the hotel - sheer luxury (hot tub) with panoramic views over Loch Ewe. Self catering if desired but only 25 yards from the main hotel. Purpose built garden barbeque for all weathers! The 'romantic theme' certainly extends to the dining room - candle-lit tables with terrific sunsets over the loch. The kitchen is fully operational with John Moir 'at the helm'. Known to me personally, his culinary talents are not unknown and he produces some fantastic meals. This rugged area of Wester Ross is one which attracts many hill visitors - Loch Maree nearby with towering hills is one of the best in Scotland. This is a real family run hotel - Peter, Margaret, Elizabeth and Mhairi Harrison together with John Moir form the perfect team and hosts. Otters and seals abound. Highly recommended.

Open: *Closed Mondays only*	**Swimming Pool/Health Club:** *No*
No. Rooms: *5 Suites; 1 single; 1 double*	**Conference Facilities:** *No*
Room telephones: *Yes*	**Price Guide:** *Single £150.00 Double £225.00 - £295.00*
TV in Rooms: *Yes*	*Dinner £48.00*
Pets: *No* **Children:** *Over 18*	*Potager £1200.00 per week (3&4 day stay available)*
Disabled: *Limited*	**Location:** *Next to Inverewe Gardens.*

Scottish Tourist Board ★★★★★ GUEST ACCOMMODATION
GOLD

BY APPOINTMENT TO H.R.H.
THE PRINCE OF WALES
PURVEYORS OF CHAMPAGNE
CHAMPAGNE LAURENT-PERRIER

BRUT L-P

DEPUIS 1812 SINCE

Laurent-Perrie

CHAMPAGNE

ÉLABORÉ PAR LAURENT-PERRIER · TOURS-SUR-MARNE · FRAN
BRUT · PRODUCE OF FRANCE · NM-235-001

DRYBURGH ABBEY HOTEL

St. Boswells, Melrose, Roxburghshire. TD6 0RQ
Tel: 01835 822261 Fax: 01835 823945
Email: enquiries@dryburgh.co.uk www.dryburgh.co.uk

Nestling in a magnificent wooded private estate on the banks of the River Tweed and immediately adjacent to the historic Dryburgh Abbey, Dryburgh Abbey Hotel commands a stunning position with magnificent views in the heart of the borders. This Scottish baronial mansion dates from the 19th century. Superior bedrooms are spacious, attractively decorated with every comfort one would expect and nice 'extra touches' - some with panoramic views. The walled garden, which is quite a feature, has been developed to produce fresh seasonal vegetables. The 2 AA rosette restaurant under the supervision of head chef Peter Snelgar is a testament to his dedicated approach and technical skills. Meals can be taken informally in the lounge or bistro area or more formally in the Tweed Restaurant on the first floor. Don't forget the indoor pool - ideal after a day filled with walking, fishing, touring, sporting or just relaxing by the pool itself. Sir Walter Scott's name is synonymous with this part of the Scottish borders – also renowned for its agriculture and rugby! Ideal venue for corporate matters ('away from it all') or weddings - just an hour's drive down the A68 from Edinburgh. Your host: Mark Wallace.

Open: *All year*	**Disabled:** *Yes*
No. Rooms: *38 (all En Suite)*	**Swimming Pool/Sauna:** *Yes*
Room telephones: *Yes*	**Conference Facilities:** *Yes*
TV in Rooms: *Yes*	**Price Guide:** *£65.00 - £186.00 (Lady of Mertoun Suite) p.p.p.n.*
Pets: *Yes*	*Enquire about seasonal breaks*
Children: *Yes*	**Location:** *2 miles from St. Boswells, Scottish Borders.*

AA ❀ ❀

FORSS HOUSE HOTEL

Forss, By Thurso, Caithness. KW14 7XY
Tel: 01847 861201 Fax: 01847 861301
Email: anne@forsshousehotel.co.uk www.forsshousehotel.co.uk

Forss House nestles in 20 acres of woodland beside a picturesque water mill just 4 miles outside Thurso. Stayed here over a 15 year period and have witnessed the progress made at this property. All main hotel bedrooms have been refurbished to an extremely high standard – obviously, a professional input that is evident with the quality of furnishings and fabrics. Large en suite bathrooms a delight. There are 4 de-luxe bedrooms within the grounds of the hotel - suit the slightly disabled with parking at your front door. The 2 AA rosettes indicate a clear ambition to achieve high standards of cuisine. Seasonal and fresh produce used - culinary skills of head chef and namesake Gary Stevenson do the rest. Breakfast taken in an attractive conservatory setting (9am deadline!). Great ambience from the pre-dinner drink through to the coffee. Cocktail bar boasts over 300 malts and there is a function suite that can take up to 14 for private dinners etc. Gillsbay ferry to Orkney is 'just down the road' as is John O'Groats and Castle of Mey, Plenty to do here – stay a bit longer this time and enjoy. Your host of many years and well known to all: Anne Mackenzie.

Open: *All year (closed 23rd Dec – 4th Jan)* **Disabled:** *Limited*
No. Rooms: *14 En Suite 14* **Swimming Pool/Health Club:** *No*
Room telephones: *Yes* **Conference Facilities:** *Up to 20*
TV in Rooms: *Yes* **Price Guide:** *Single from £100.00 - £135.00*
Pets: *Yes* *Double from £135.00 - £185.00*
Children: *Yes* **Location:** *4 miles from Thurso on A836*

AA ❀ ❀

TIRORAN HOUSE HOTEL

Tiroran, Isle of Mull, Argyll. PA69 6ES
Tel: 01681 705232
Email: info@tiroran.com www.tiroran.com

If you are going to Mull this is certainly the place to stay – absolutely stunning loch side views and property. The gardens are truly magnificent with well manicured lawns overlooking Loch Scridain. A real paradise. I discovered Tiroran over 20 years ago and was delighted to return. Situated 4 miles off the 'main road' on the south part of the island it's a short hop to Iona and trips to Staffa. Laurence & Katie Mackay arrived here in 2004 and describe Tiroran as a boutique hotel – ideal for that discerning visitor – bedrooms are just so comfortable (king size beds) with a lot of extra touches and extremely well furnished. Excellent en suite facilities. Pre-dinner drinks with Laurence in the drawing room sets the tone in the evening. Under the expert supervision of Katie the cuisine was a gastronomic delight. Good use of fresh produce - some from loch to table. Organic garden. Dedication here and a real effort with the comfort of the guest in mind. Although a hotel, it's really a charming home with terrific ambience. There are 2 self catering cottages on the property. A real wildlife experience with sea & golden eagles, otters and whale watching. A climb up Ben More (a Munro) or a visit to Duart Castle could be an option. Linger awhile at Tiroran and indulge yourself. Equi-distant from Iona and Tobermory. Highly recommended.

Open: *April - November*	**Swimming Pool/Health Club:** *No*
No. Rooms: *9 En Suite 9*	**Conference Facilities:** *No*
Room telephones: *No*	**Price Guide:** *Single from £110.00 Double £165.00 - £200.00*
TV in Rooms: *Yes*	*King size and superking beds (also twins) available*
Pets: *Arrangement* **Children:** *Over 12* **Location:**	*Craignure-Iona ferry road south. Turn off at Kinloch*
Disabled: *Limited*	*onto the B8035 for 4 miles.*

THE TORRIDON
Torridon, Wester Ross IV22 2EY
Tel: 01445 791242
Email: info@thetorridon.com www.thetorridon.com

An outstanding Victorian baronial mansion (circa 1887) in a spectacular highland setting with magnificent views over Loch Torridon to the mountains beyond. Just be careful on the single track road whether approaching from Kinlochewe or from Kyle of Lochalsh – just take in the scenery in one of the most beautiful areas of North East Scotland. The property was built by the Earl of Lovelace in the grand style of the day and this theme has been retained throughout the hotel and garden policies. My first overnight stay here was in 1994 (except in earlier years with my parents) 2 years after the Gregory Family moved from Kinlochbervie Hotel and initiated a programme to overhaul and refurbish this great property. Latterly it has been operated by their daughter Rohaise and husband Daniel Rose-Bristow and now ranks as one of the premier hotels in the country. All bedrooms whether classic or superior/master are luxurious in all aspects. The technical skills of head chef Bruno Birbeck are to be admired (and enjoyed). This is a first class culinary operation which reflects the 3 AA rosette award. The ambience of the wood panelled dining room just perfect. The Torridon Inn nearby provides an option to dine in a more informal setting (Bistro). Activity destination with archery, falconry, stalking, hill climbing and water sports. Corporate enquiries welcome and maybe even a small exclusive wedding. Voted AA Scottish Hotel of the Year 2012-2013.

Open: *All year ex. 4 weeks January*	**Swimming Pool/Health Club:** *No*
No. Rooms: *18 En Suite 18*	**Conference Facilities:** *16 Director level*
Room telephones: *Yes*	**Price Guide:** *Double £220.00 - £455.00 (suite)*
TV in Rooms: *Yes*	*Tariff depends on season & length of stay.*
Pets: *Yes - in cottage* **Children:** *Yes*	**Location:**
Disabled: *Yes*	*Inverness - Achnasheen. Take A832 to Kinlochewe village. Take turning clearly marked Torridon 10 miles.*

FARLAM HALL

Brampton, Cumbria. CA8 2NG
Tel: 016977 46234   Fax: 016977 46683
Email: farlam@relaischateaux.com   www.farlamhall.co.uk

This is truly a magnificent 17th century ivy clad country manor set amongst wonderful parkland – a member of the prestigious Relais & Chateaux no less. The lake and fountain to the front are remarkable features – from the moment you arrive and enter Farlam Hall there is an atmosphere of peace and contentment. A stroll in the gardens with afternoon tea sets the tone – bedrooms are extremely comfortable – spacious (large windows) and well furnished complimented by large en suite bathrooms. This was my 8th overnight stay at Farlam Hall - a most enjoyable experience on every occasion. The programme of upgrading continues at Farlam in keeping with this manor house of great character. The Quinion family have owned Farlam Hall since 1975 and the finest traditions of hotel keeping are evident. The comfort of the guest is paramount. Add to this the fine cuisine and attentive service and you have the complete product. Daily-changing menus - a great dining experience. All fresh ingredients, carefully sourced and so well executed by chef Barry Quinion. Home made desserts 'to die for'. Just 'over the border' this is an ideal stop whether travelling north or south. Hadrian's Wall and many other historical sites closeby. Go for it, indulge yourself. 2 AA food rosettes and 3 AA red stars.

Open: *All year ex. 24th-31st Dec; 3rd-10th Jan*	**Swimming Pool/Health Club:** *No*
No. Rooms: *12 En Suite 12*	**Conference Facilities:** *Up to 12 director level*
Room telephones: *Yes*	**Price Guide:** *Single £160.00 - £190.00 dinner, b&b*
TV in Rooms: *Yes*	*Double £300.00 - £360.00 dinner, b&b*
Pets: *Yes* **Children:** *Over 5*	**Location:** *Junction 43 on M6. 12 miles on A689 to*
Disabled: *Not suitable*	*Alston. Not in Farlam village.*

MALLORY COURT

Harbury Lane, Leamington Spa, Warwickshire. CV33 9QB
Tel: 01926 330214   Fax: 01926 415714
email: reception@mallory.co.uk   www.mallory.co.uk

Mallory Court Hotel is a breathtakingly beautiful country house hotel, set in 10 acres of gardens and just outside Leamington Spa, Warwickshire. A member of the prestigious Relais & Chateaux group it has already been recognised by the AA as one of their top hotels in the country. In addition, with head chef Nigel Haighe (ex Inverlochy Castle) 'at the helm' it has been awarded a **Michelin Star** for a number of years. The Michelin rated hotel already holds 3 AA rosettes for the main Dining Room but now the Brasserie at Mallory has been recognised by the AA with the award of 2 rosettes. This elegant, Lutens-style country manor house is quite the little piece of England; an idyllic, impeccable retreat set in 10 acres of landscaped grounds and immaculate lawns. Contemporary country house splendour is the style, where pampered relaxation comes easy in sumptuous lounges over aperitifs or coffee, the mellow, homely atmosphere cultivated by an efficient, dedicated and enthusiastic team. Part of the Eden Collection - see website for more information.

Open: *All year*	**Disabled:** *1 room designated (lift access)*
No. Rooms: *30*	**Swimming Pool/Health Club:** *Yes*
Room telephones: *Yes*	**Conference Facilities:** *Excellent - up to 160*
TV in Rooms: *Yes*	**Price Guide:** *£125.00 - £395.00*
Pets: *Arrangement*	**Location:** *M40 from London, Jct. 13; from Birmingham*
Children: *Yes*	*Jct. 14. 2 mls. on B4087 to Leamington Spa.*

MARLFIELD HOUSE

Gorey, Co. Wexford, Ireland.
Tel: (00353) 5394 21124   Fax: (00353) 5394 21572
Email: info@marlfieldhouse.ie   www.marlfieldhouse.com

Once again I am delighted to include Marlfield House as my Irish 'Associate Hotel' for edition 2013. It came strongly recommended and is a member of the prestigious Relais & Chateaux group. Formerly the residence of the Earls of Courtown Marlfield House is a very elegant 19th. century mansion set in its own grounds of wonderful garden, woodland and parkland policies. The State Rooms are decorated with rich fabrics and fine antique furniture - all have period marble fireplaces and elegant marble bathrooms. Every room is spacious and offers every luxury. The interior of the hotel is resplendent with fine paintings and antiques and the conservatory is a feature overlooking the garden. Cuisine described as 'classical with a French and Mediterranean influence' which has been awarded 3 AA red rosettes for food. The Bowe family are to be congratulated on keeping the standards of yesterday today. To maintain such high standards is testament to a firm commitment and dedication. Relais & Chateaux member since 1984. 3 AA red stars. General Managers: Margaret and Laura Bowe.

Open: *All year exc. Jan 2nd - mid Feb.*	**Disabled:** *Limited*
No. Rooms: *13 (6 suites) En Suite 13*	**Swimming Pool/Health Club:** *No*
Room telephones: *Yes*	**Conference Facilities:** *Small - Director Level*
TV in Rooms: *Yes*	**Price Guide:** *Double. Room - Standard: Euro 230 - 260*
Pets: *Arrangement*	*State Rooms: Euro 370 - 650 (Master)*
Children: *Yes*	**Location:** *80 km south of Dublin*

AA ✿✿✿
★★★

YNYSHIR HALL

Eglwysfach, Machynlleth, Powys, SY20 8TA

Tel: 01654 781209   Fax: 01654 781366

email: info@ynyshir-hall.co.uk   www.ynyshir-hall.co.uk

Another member of the prestigious Relais & Chateaux (since 2001) this is certainly one for the connoisseur. Managed and hosted for many years by Rob and Joan Reen it is the epitomy of the finest standards of hotel keeping. Delightful 16th century manor house surrounded by magnificent gardens - opulence and gracious living on a fine scale - the perfect 'hideaway' in the west of Wales near Aberwyswyth. The 9 bedrooms which include 2 suites are perfectly appointed - large with antique beds and furniture to complement. Rob and Joan have used their immense talents (Rob is an artist) to create interiors which express warmth, elegance and charm. The AA 3 red rosette award for food demonstrates a high commitment in achieving high standards of cuisine using high quality suppliers with fresh seasonal produce. Excellent technical skills successfully executed. Cocktail bar with log fire and restaurant with fine linen and glassware allied with an excellent wine list is the complete dining experience. Ideal location for a visit to the Dovey estuary - one of the finest bird reserves in the country.

Open: *All year*	**Disabled:** *1 room*
No. Rooms: *9 (2 suites) En Suite 9*	**Swimming Pool/Health Club:** *No*
Room telephones: *Yes*	**Conference Facilities:** *Director level 25*
TV in Rooms: *Yes*	**Price Guide:** *Double £325.00 - £345.00*
Pets: *1 room only*	*Suites £375.00 - £405.00*
Children: *Over 9*	**Location:** *10 miles from Aberwystwyth.*

AA ✿✿✿
★★★

STEVENSONS

SCOTLAND'S
GOOD FOOD BOOK WITH RECIPES
2013

Photo by kind permission of Greywalls Hotel & Chez Roux

STEVENSONS

SCOTLAND'S
GOOD FOOD BOOK
2013

FOREWORD

I feel not only honoured but also extremely privileged to be writing the foreword for Alan Stevenson's wonderful book. Alan's book has always been one that I have personally enjoyed reading and I have found his knowledge to be greatly useful and which I am sure it will continue to be in the future.

I returned home to Scotland in April 2010 to open Greywalls Hotel & Chez Roux Restaurant under the guidance of the legendary Albert Roux. It had been the most amazing experience working for Mr Roux at his London based restaurant Le Gavroche, but I felt the time was right to return home to Scotland.

Our style at Chez Roux is very much classical French with the use of modern techniques and contemporary presentation.

Greywalls Hotel really could not be situated in a more beautiful part of the country. East Lothian has been blessed in terms of quality of produce and quantity of local suppliers. The surrounding water is packed with lobsters, crabs & langoustine which are always of the highest quality. Pedigree Aberdeen Angus, free range wild boar and wonderful young lamb are all reared locally. In the season the Scottish Borders provides us with an abundance of wild game which I enjoy using extensively on our menu at Chez Roux.

A large part of Greywalls Hotel's beauty lies within Mrs Weaver's beautiful garden. On a summers day this is an unbelievable place to visit. Along with its natural beauty and character the garden produces a vast amount of the freshest and most wonderful produce. Honey is produced here from our own bee hives and the most beautiful vibrant eggs laid by the free range hens.

I am extremely proud of my team's achievements since the opening and with everyone's hard work and dedication I look forward to the future with Chez Roux at Greywalls Hotel.

Derek Johnstone - Head Chef
Greywalls & Chez Roux Restaurant
Muirfield, Gullane, East Lothian
Tel: 01620 842144
chef@greywalls.co.uk

Derek Johnstone - Head Chef
Greywalls & Chez Roux Restaurant

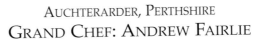

RESTAURANT ANDREW FAIRLIE

AUCHTERARDER, PERTHSHIRE
GRAND CHEF: ANDREW FAIRLIE

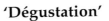

'Dégustation'

Tomato, Crab, Aubergine

Ballotine of Foie Gras
Peach Carpaccio and Almond Milk

Roast Hand Dived Scallops
Squid Cracker

Parmessan and Truffle Grattin
Girolles and Jus Gras

Home Smoked Scottish Lobster
Warm Lime and Herb Butter

Slow Cooked Spring Lamb
Romesco Sauce

Ages Comté
Urban Honey

Raspberries
Rose Water Meringue

Coffee and Chocolates

Price: £125.00
Wine Cellar to Match

THE CONSERVATORY
(THE MARCLIFFE HOTEL, SPA AND RESTAURANT)
North Deeside Road, Aberdeen. AB15 9YA
Tel: 01224 861000 Fax: 01224 868860
Email: reservations@marcliffe.com www.marcliffe.com

The Marcliffe Hotel has all the attributes of a first class operation including the Conservatory Restaurant which forms an integral part of the overall experience (also see hotel entry on page 15). Dined here on many an occasion and love the experience – large open conservatory setting with clothed tables and very efficient staff. Bespoke a la carte menu which includes wonderful fish, meat and game dishes. Seafood (crab and lobster) a speciality. Quality suppliers clearly indicated on the menu – only the very best of produce used here. Executive Chef Michael Stoddart and Head Chef Ross Spence should be proud of their achievements and their talents are obvious – consistent throughout. Fantastic wine cellar. An outstanding breakfast menu for which I would award a mark of 10/10. Great ambience. Front of house operation faultless. Ideal for that special occasion in perfect surroundings. Aberdeen airport 25 minutes. Ample car parking.

Open: *All year*	**Disabled:**	*Yes*
No Rooms: *42 ensuite*	**Price Guide:**	*Same a la carte menu for lunch*
TV in Rooms: *Yes*		*and dinner £25.00 - £65.00*
Room Tel. *Yes*	**Location:**	*Aberdeen ring road. Turn west at A93*
Children: *Yes*		*to Braemar. 1 mile on right*

RESTAURANT ANDREW FAIRLIE
The Gleneagles Hotel, Auchterarder, Perthshire. PH3 1NF
Tel: 01764 694267 Fax: 01764 694163.
Email: andrew.fairlie@gleneagles.com www.andrewfairlie.com

Now a member of the prestigious Relais & Chateaux and installed as Grand Chef Andrew Fairlie displays a real passion for food. He is driven by innovation, evolving ideas and new concepts and his technical skills are obvious. Located at the iconic Gleneagles Hotel, in this beautiful part of Perthshire, my 10th visit was once again the complete dining experience. Style of cooking can be described as classical French with a contemporary twist. Sophisticated menus (a la carte, du Marche and degustation) with carefully sourced ingredients from moor and glen, local farms and fish from the famous River Tay. Foraging for chanterelles and wild berries. Great ambience and a very fine wine cellar. Front of house operation, under the care of Ben Dantzic, is one of the best. This is one for the connoisseur. Multi awarded restaurant with **2 Michelin Stars** and 4 AA rosettes. A wonderful testimonial for the Scottish culinary industry. *AA*

Open: *All year (Dinner only) ex 3wks Jan. Closed Sun.*	**Disabled:**	*Unsuitable*
No Rooms: *N/A*	**Covers:**	*56*
TV in Rooms: *N/A*	**Price Guide:**	*£85.00 - £125.00*
Room Tel. *N/A*		*Cheese £14.00 Coffee £5.00*
Children: *Over 12*	**Location:**	*Ground floor of Gleneagles Hotel.*

KINLOCH LODGE
SLEAT, ISLE OF SKYE
HEAD CHEF: MARCELLO TULLY

Slightly spicy pea soupcon
Wine Flight Z £32.00 (2 small glasses - 125mls each):
TAITTINGER BRUT RÉSERVE N.V.;
BOLLINGER SPECIAL CUVEE N.V.

**Steamed Mallaig cod,
caramelised grapefruit**
Wine Flight Z as above

**Roast quail, vegetable and Perthshire honey mousse,
cauliflower, port and orange jus**
Wine Flight X £24.00 (2 small glasses - 125mls each):
CLOUDY BAY SAUVIGNON BLANC, MARLBOROUGH 2010;
CAPE MENTELLE CHARDONNAY, MARGARET RIVER 2006

**Slow roast Moray pork belly, seared west coast scallops,
sweet pickled fennel, oriental sauce**
Wine Flight Y £28.00 (2 small glasses - 125mls each):
CLOUDY BAY PINOT NOIR, MARLBOROUGH 2008;
NUMANTHIA, TORO 2007

**Strathdon blue cheese, prune and orange mousse,
Perthshire honey jellies**
Wine Flight Y as above

**Rich dark chocolate,
basil espuma**
Wine Flight ZZ £20.00 (2 at 50mls each):
VIN DE CONSTANCE, KLEIN CONSTANTIA, 2007;
NOBLE ROT SEMILLON, HENSCHKE, EDEN VALLEY 2008

**Scottish rhubarb crumble
rhubarb ice cream**
Wine Flight ZZ as above

Coffee and homemade petits fours,
served in the drawing rooms

TASTING MENU - £75 PER PERSON
(To be taken by everyone at the table)
£10 supplement for residents on a dinner bed and breakfast tariff

Wine flights are individually priced
or why not share all four flights for £95

TASTING MENU

KINLOCH LODGE

Sleat, Isle of Skye, Inverness-shire. IV43 8QY

Tel: 01471 833333 Fax: 01471 833277

Email: reservations@kinloch-lodge.co.uk www.kinloch-lodge.co.uk

Returned for two visits this year and enjoyed the company of **Michelin Star** chef Marcello Tully and his award winning cuisine. The experience here is quite exceptional and if time wasn't always against me I would dine here more often. A culinary triumph once again - vibrant flavours, innovation and a bit of flair (see tasting menu opposite) allied with high technical skills produces a wonderful dining experience. Wine cellar of note and a great ambience within this island hotel. This is the home of Lady Claire Macdonald (see main Foreword) and her husband Lord Godfrey. Their daughter Isabella & husband Tom have now taken over 'the reins' and although the food and beverage operation is of great importance there are 15 en suite bedrooms furnished to an extremely high standard. Wonderful views over to Knoydart and Mallaig. No rush here – just enjoy and indulge yourself. **Michelin Star** and 3 AA rosettes. Highly recommended. ***AA*** 🏵🏵🏵 🍲

Open: *All year*	**Price Guide:** *Lunch £29.99 (2 courses)*	
No Rooms: *15 ensuite*	*£34.99 (3 courses)*	
TV in Rooms: *Yes* **Room Tel.** *Yes*	*Dinner £55.00–£65.00 (4, 5 or 6 courses)*	
Children: *Yes* **Disabled:** *1 room*	*Tasting menu £75.00*	
Covers: *36* *(ground floor)*	**Location:** *Short distance from Broadford on the Armadale Ferry road*	

BRAIDWOODS

Drumastle Mill Cottage, By Dalry, Ayrshire, KA24 4LN

Tel: 01294 833544 Fax: 01294 833553

email: keithbraidwood@btconnect.com www.braidwoods.co.uk

Michelin Star restaurant since 2000 Keith and Nicola Braidwood fully deserve the plaudits they have received over the years. Attractive converted country styled cottage surrounded by fields just outside Dalry in Ayrshire. Idyllic situation. I have known Keith and Nicola since their days at Shieldhill Country House near Biggar where their culinary efforts were also recognised. By repute expectations are high and I have never been disappointed when sampling the fayre. Great prep work and good sourcing of ingredients are obvious. High technical skills here with flair and a consistency throughout the meal. Depth of flavour evident. No restricted menu here – sophisticated and varied choice. Boneless quail stuffed with black pudding a favourite. Nicola's 'front of house' skills are exemplary – relaxed atmosphere and a warm welcome. Too many awards to mention – **Michelin Star** held for 13 years. 🍲

Open: *All year ex 3wks Jan & 2wks Sept*	**Price Guide:** *Lunch £23.00–£26.00 (2 or 3 Course)*	
Closed Sun dinner, Mon all day, Tues lunch	*Dinner £43.00–£48.00 (3 or 4 course)*	
Children: *Over 12*	*Sunday lunch £30.00 (May - September)*	
Disabled: *Not suitable*	**Location:** *Take road to Salcoats from A737 - 1 mile*	
Covers: *24*	*and follow signs.*	

THE THREE CHIMNEYS
AND THE HOUSE OVER-BY
Colbost, By Dunvegan, Isle of Skye. IV55 8ZT
Tel: 01470 511258   Fax: 01470 511358
Email: eatandstay@threechimneys.co.uk   www.threechimneys.co.uk

Winner of numerous awards Shirley and Eddie Spears have forged an oasis of culinary excellence, in the middle of nowhere, which began with the renovation of the 100 year old cottage some 27 years ago. The consistency in the standard of cuisine over the years has been extraordinary. With the introduction of 6 suites in 1999 it took on a 'new look' – and developed into a 5 star VisitScotland 'Restaurant with Rooms'. De luxe suites with small verandah and panoramic views over Loch Dunvegan. Only a short distance from Dunvegan itself the area is abundant in natural food resources – fresh fish, game, lamb and venison – seafood a speciality. Perfect dining experience brilliantly executed by Chef/Director Michael Smith. Eddie on hand with his vast knowledge of wines which adds to the experience. Situated 4 miles west of Dunvegan on the road to Glendale and under the watchful eye of the 'MacLeod Tables' you won't want to miss this one when on the Isle of Skye. **AA** ❀ ❀ ❀ 🍴

Open:	All year (ex. 2 weeks Jan)		Price Guide:	Lunch £28.50 - £37.00 Dinner £60.00 (3 courses)
No Rooms:	6 Suites			Tasting Menu £90.00 (7 courses)
TV in Rooms:	Yes			Chef's Table £100.00 with wine £150.00
Room Tel.	Yes Children: Yes		Location:	B884, 4 miles West of Dunvegan on
Disabled:	Yes			Road to Glendale

(Scottish ★★★★★ GOLD)

THE LINTON
3 Bridgend, East Linton, East Lothian. EH40 3AF
Tel: 01620 860202
Email: infolinton@aol.com   www.thelintonhotel.co.uk

An attractive 18th century rural 'restaurant with rooms' within the village of East Linton between Haddington and Dunbar. Known to me personally for over 20 years, George and Michelle Kelso relocated here some 4 years ago from the well known Haldanes restaurant in Edinburgh. Over this short time they have built up an envious reputation for quality fayre allied with a great village pub ambience. George, formerly a consistent 2 AA rosette chef, displays a mastery of all things culinary. Menus produce dishes of a sound quality, vibrant flavours and the secret – fresh ingredients from local farmers and sea outlets at Port Seton and Dunbar. As a member of The Scotch Beef Club this ensures high on quality, high on taste! Choice of 'light bite' menus to more sophisticated dishes. Sunday roast and steak suppers are a firm favourite. There are 6 en suite comfortable bedrooms and a garden area to the rear. Corporate and small wedding enquiries welcome. Area full of historical interest, popular walks and not far from the sea. Golf courses everywhere! A short drive from the city hazards of Edinburgh. 🍴

Open:	All year		Price Guide:	Rooms £30.00 - £50.00 pppn
No Rooms:	6 En Suite 6			Lunch £5.50 - £12.50
TV in Rooms:	Yes + Wifi			Dinner £10.00 - £22.00 (a la carte)
Room Tel.	Yes		Location:	Middle of village whether approaching
Children:	Yes Disabled: Dining only			from east or west

NUMBER ONE RESTAURANT

1, Princes Street, Edinburgh. EH2 2EQ
Tel : 0131 557 6727   Fax : 0131 557 3747
Email : numberone@thebalmoralhotel.com   www.roccofortehotels.com

Dinner at Number One is indeed a wonderful dining experience. One for 'the foodies' of that there is no doubt. Although part of The Balmoral Hotel the restaurant has created a reputation in its own right for fine dining - executive chef Jeff Bland whose culinary expertise is well known displays a quality of skills which have brought him recognition from many agencies and a number of awards. Jeff is equally at home with modern or traditional dishes - good combinations showing flair and imagination. High technical skills with some innovation, good texture and taste. There can be no doubt that diners' expectations are fully realised - also a fine wine list available for the connoisseur. Ambience perfect with fine furnishings and white linen - sound advice and service impeccable. **Michelin Star**. Restaurant Manager: Gary Quinn. *AA* 🌸 🌸 🌸 🍽

Open:	Closed first 2 weeks January	Disabled:	Access available
	Monday - Sunday: 6pm - 10.30pm	Covers:	55
No Rooms:	188	Price Guide:	3 course a la carte £64 (excluding wine)
TV in Rooms: Yes	Room Tel. Yes		Chef's Tasting Menu £70 (add £55 for wine pairings)
Children:	Yes	Location:	1 Princes Street

STAC POLLY RESTAURANT

29-33 Dublin Street, Edinburgh. EH3 6NL.
Tel: 0131 556 2231   Fax: 0131 557 9779.
www.stacpolly.co.uk

Charismatic owner Roger Coulthard, whom I have known for over twenty years, is a serious player in the culinary circles of Edinburgh. From a humble beginning at Dublin Street many years ago Roger eventually expanded his business and can also be found in St. Mary's Street not far from the Royal Mile. The name Stac Polly comes from the famous Scottish mountain on the west coast of Scotland north of Ullapool. The restaurant maintains the Scottish theme throughout with tartan draperies and colour schemes that reflect heather clad hills that recall highland clans. The cuisine is mainly Scottish with slight European influences. Menus are compiled using the finest and freshest of Scottish produce creating dishes that are innovative with flair and imagination which is prevalent throughout. Specialities include filo pastry parcels of haggis served on a sweet plum and coriander jus. Other favourites include gressingham duck, seabass, saddle of venison, fillet of Scottish beef and loin of lamb. Always enjoyed my meals here over the years and have received very good 'feedback' on both establishments. *AA* 🌸

Open:	All year	Disabled:	Unsuitable
No Rooms:	N/A	Covers:	40
TV in Rooms:	N/A	Price Guide:	Lunch: 2 courses £12.00-£15.00 (2 courses)
Room Tel.	N/A		Dinner: £25.00-£32.00 (3 courses)
Children:	Yes	Location:	Nr St Andrews Square. New Town - Central

EAT ON THE GREEN
UDNY GREEN, ABERDEENSHIRE
CHEF / PROPRIETOR: CRAIG WILSON

TASTING MENU

Champagne and Oysters

Amuse-Bouche

Roasted Quail, Braised Oxtail, Blueberry Jus
COTE DE RHONE ROUGE, CHATEAU MONT REDON, RHONE 2010 – 100ML

Hand Dived Scallops, Confit Chicken Wings, Périgourdine Sauce
CHARDONNAY, MOUNTADAM, AUSTRALIA 2010 – 100ML

Mackerel, White Chocolate, Horseradish, Beetroot
GAVI, CAMPOROSSO 2009 – 100ML

Roasted Sweetcorn, Tomato and Basil Risotto
TORRONTES, FINCA LA FLORENCIA, FAMILIA CASSONE, ARGENTINA 2010 – 100ML

Duo of Lamb Sweetbreads, Pea and Truffle Salad, Mushroom Veloute
PINOT NOIR, PENCARROW ESTATE, NEW ZEALAND 2010

Fillet of Beef, Confit Foie Gras, Sweet Potato Fondant, Sour Cherry
SYRAH, RUDI SCHULTZ, STELLENBOSCH 2008 – 125ML

Butter Braised Lobster, Crispy Chicken and Sage Terrine, Tempura Claw, Spring Onion Mash
FLEURIE VIEILLES VIGNES, POTEL-AVIRON, BEAUJOLAIS 2009– 125ML

Rosemary Roasted Peaches, Almond Milk Ice Cream, Citrus Biscotti

Bitter Chocolate Delice, Sherry Caramel, Orange
CHATEAU PETIT VEDRINES, SAUTERNES 2008 – 100ML

Selection of European Cheese (£10 Supplement)
DELAFORCE PORT 10 YEAR OLD TAWNY– 50ML

TASTING MENU £95.00 PER PERSON
WITH PAIRED WINES £125.00 PER PERSON

EAT ON THE GREEN

Udny Green, Ellon, Aberdeenshire. AB41 7RS

Tel: 01651 842337 Fax: 01651 843362
Email: enquiries@eatonthegreen.co.uk www.eatonthegreen.co.uk

A fantastic rural location overlooking the village green at Udny Green not far from Ellon and close to the famous Pitmedden Gardens. My annual visit here just gets better and better and this was another culinary triumph allied with a good natter with a very enthusiastic chef / proprietor Craig Wilson. His energy levels are beyond me but his pure passion for food propels him in all his endeavours. There is a clear ambition to achieve high standards here – this year he has introduced a terrific tasting menu (see opposite) of 10 courses for the 'real foodie' or for everyone in fact. Quality sourcing of ingredients from what can only be described as a natural larder in this rich part of agricultural Aberdeenshire and fish from the local harbour. Perfect dining experience from start to finish with a very efficient 'Front of House' operation. Celebrity visitors include the First Minister Alex Salmond and culinary awards have followed. Phone reservations advisable. Awarded 2 AA rosettes and member of The Scotch Beef Club. *AA* 🏵 🏵 🏆

Open: *Closed Mon/Tues*	**Price Guide:** *Lunch: £22.00 - £25.00 (Weekdays)*
Children: *Yes*	*Lunch: £25.00 - £30.00 (Sundays)*
Disabled: *Yes* **Covers:** *80*	*Sat. Eve. £52.00 (4 courses - set price)*
Location: *A920 from Ellon. B999 from*	*Tasting Menu £95 (£125 with matched wine)*
Aberdeen. (Nr Pitmedden Gardens)	*Afternoon Tea £18 (£27 with glass champagne)*

STRAVAIGIN

28 Gibson Street, Hillhead, Glasgow. G12 8NX

Tel: 0141 334 2665 Fax: 0141 334 4099.
Email: bookings@stravaigin.com www.stravaigin.com

Now a household name in Glasgow Stravaigin has taken on a 'new look' – the traditional Scottish roots are still apparent with the introduction of a more classical and contempory style. Difficult to describe the ambience here – certainly different and unusual. Bistro bordering on fine dining with some really wonderful combinations. Chilean stew of seafood and meats with Scottish mussels, lamb and rabbit. Aberdeen Angus sirloin topped with cajun styled prawns could be your choice. Catering for an ever evolving customer who require something different it has become more evident over the years that tastes and trends are changing. Stravaigin has introduced this innovative style of fusion which attracts its faithful followers. Good 'front of house' with staff who have been here for a few years and an extensive wine cellar add to the dining experience. Good value for money. 🏆

Open: *All year ex. Xmas, New Year & Sundays*	**Covers:** *76*
No Rooms: *N/A*	**Price Guide:** *Dinner: from £34.00 (3 courses)*
TV in Rooms: *N/A* **Room Tel.** *N/A*	*Lunch: from £12.95*
Children: *Yes*	**Location:** *M8, junct 17 or A82 from city centre - Gt Western*
Disabled: *Unsuitable*	*road, turn down park road, rt into Gibson St., 200 yds on right*

ABSTRACT RESTAURANT & BRASSERIE

20 Ness Bank, Inverness. IV2 4SF
Tel: 01463 223777 Fax: 01463 712378
Email: reception@glenmoristontownhouse.com www.abstractrestaurant.com

An attractive situation on the banks of the River Ness this restaurant is an integral part of The Glenmoriston Town House. There are a number of really good restaurants in Inverness and this is one of them. Known to me over a number of years now there has always been a desire to produce a wonderful dining experience. On my visits the high standards and technical skills are obvious. Great combinations which are quite exciting and different. Choice of 7 course tasting menu. Chef's table in the kitchen an exciting innovation. Sophiscated menus and excellent wine cellar. You can also dine (alfresco in the Summer months) more informally in the delightful Contrast Brasserie. Over 250 malt whiskies on display in the Piano bar. Great ambience and professional 'front of house' operation. Ample car parking.***AA***

Open: *All year*		**Disabled:**	*Yes*
No Rooms: 30		**Covers:**	*35*
TV in Rooms: *Yes*		**Price Guide:**	*Dinner from £45.00*
Room Tel. *Yes*			*Tasting Menu from £65.00*
Children: *Yes*		**Location:**	*Ness Bank 5 minutes from City Centre*

CHEZ ROUX RESTAURANT

Rocpool Reserve, Culduthel Road, Inverness. IV2 4AG
Tel: 01463 240089 Fax: 01463 248431
email: info@rocpool.com www.rocpool.com

To quote Albert Roux, "I want to create the kind of restaurant I remember from my home town, offering good and honest country cooking. The kind of place you can go to eat without ringing the bank for permission. Chez Roux will offer Scottish ingredients with a 'French Twist.' This is exactly what I experienced during my visit – creative and imaginative dishes, perfectly executed with faultless presentation. Exciting flavours (pike quenelle with lobster sauce a firm favourite) dominate – fish of the day & meat of the day are standard options from the a la carte with sensible combinations. However, menus offer an excellent choice. Wonderful puddings. All, I should add, at a very modest price. Elegant and extremely comfortable dining room with views over the city. I would recommend The Chez Roux experience to everyone. Go for it. Chef Albert Roux OBE, KFO, is head of the famous cooking dynasty behind such establishments as Le Gavroche which was the first restaurant in the UK to be awarded three Michelin Stars.

Open: *All year*		**Disabled:**	*Yes*
No Rooms: 11		**Covers:**	*32*
TV in Rooms: *Yes*		**Price Guide:**	*Lunch: £12.50 - £25.00*
Room Tel. *Yes*			*Dinner: £15.00 - £30.00*
Children: *Over 8*		**Location:**	*Culduthel Road, just up from Inverness Castle.*

FULLY INTEGRATED SOLUTIONS

Brodies offer a fully integrated coffee solution with a range of coffees roasted in our factory in Musselburgh matched to a comprehensive range of coffee machines from filter, to traditional & bean to cup machines.

We also blend a range of speciality teas and infusions and premium quality catering teas.

Our range includes a selection of In-room hospitality products as well as a comprehensive range of Fairtrade products.

Max Hogg & Brigade
Livingston's Restaurant

See recipe on pages 90-91

THE GROUSE AND CLARET RESTAURANT

Heatheryford, Kinross. KY13 0NQ
Tel: 01577 864212 Fax: 01577 864920
Email: grouseandclaret@lineone.net www.grouseandclaret.com

The Grouse and Claret is really a country centre which combines accommodation, an art gallery and a fishery. It is very conveniently situated just off the M90 between Edinburgh and Perth in a rural setting - in fact there are 25 acres encompassing restaurant, art gallery, fishery and meadow. A permanent fixture here for many years chef proprietor David Futong and his wife Vicki have earned an enviable reputation for quality cuisine in an ideal setting. Absolutely delightful dining room setting within the conservatory with views over the meadow. Menus are sensible and cater for all tastes - great emphasis on delicious home made food, beautifully presented. This is a wonderful setting for small weddings and functions. Comfortable detached bedrooms - some overlooking the trout ponds make this the ideal base in the country only a short drive from the city hazards of Edinburgh. Ample car parking.

Open: *All year ex. 1 wk. Jan; 10 days Oct. Sun. night/all day Mon.*	**Disabled:** *Yes*	**Covers:** *60*	
No Rooms: *3 En Suite 3*	**Price Guide:** *B&B price per room: Double: £80.00; Single: £50.00 Lunch £10.50 - £20.00 Dinner £20.00 - £35.00 (à la carte)*		
TV in Rooms: *Yes* **Room Tel.** *No*	**Location:** *Leave M90 Junction (6) then 500 yds - Private Road Opposite Service Station*		
Children: *Yes*			

LIVINGSTON'S RESTAURANT

52 High Street, Linlithgow, West Lothian. EH49 7AE
Tel: 01506 846565
Email: contact@livingstons-restaurant.co.uk www.livingstons-restaurant.co.uk

This is what you call a real hidden gem of a restaurant. A 'cottage' themed restaurant set in attractive gardens it is located through a vennel off the main street. The new extension fits in perfectly with the original rustic type dining room. A family business in the true sense of the word, this is a great success story which has been built up by the Livingston family over a number of years. No compromise here - consistently high strandards of cuisine coupled with excellent front of house service. Excellent choice and combinations with vibrant flavours. Menu always changing to reflect the good use of seasonal fresh produce. Wine cellar of note. A thriving restaurant with a high percentage of repeat business. Once you have visited you will return. Even just to taste Christine Livingston's tablet! Your hosts: Ronald, Christine and Derek Livingston. *AA* ❀❀❀

Open: *Closed Sun/Mon & 1st 2 weeks Jan and 1 week June & Oct*	**Disabled:** *Yes*	**Covers:** *50*	
No Rooms: *N/A*	**Price Guide:** *Lunch £16.95 - £19.95 Dinner £32.95 (2 courses) Dinner £38.95 (3 courses)*		
TV in Rooms: *N/A* **Room Tel.** *N/A*			
Children: *Over 8 (evening)*	**Location:** *Eastern end of High Street opp. Post Office.*		

TAYCHREGGAN HOTEL

Kilchrenan, By Taynuilt, Argyll. PA35 1HQ
Tel: 01866 833211/366 Fax: 01866 833244
Email: info@taychregganhotel.co.uk www.taychregganhotel.com

My association with this hotel goes back to the halcyon days of 1988! It commands one of the best spots in Scotland on the side of Loch Awe. An inspired position. After a lot of hard work and perseverence these halcyon days are returning under the stewardship of General Manager Fiona Sutherland. Finally, all bedrooms, whether standard, superior or master suite have been completely upgraded with no expense spared. De luxe quality throughout. The dining room, with awesome views over the Loch are breathtaking. The kitchen brigade produce mouth watering dishes making good use of all the natural seasonal ingredients available on his doorstep. Ambience just perfect and service faultless. Spacious & very comfortable lounge areas with cosy fire in the winter months. Clearly signposted from just before the village of Taynuilt take care on the 8 mile single track road – quite an adventure in itself! There is even falconry and clay pigeon shooting available on the grounds. Enquiries for seasonal 'breaks' and weddings welcome. **AA** 🏵🏵 🍴

Open: *All year*	**Price Guide:**	*Double £126.00 - £301.00 (Master Suite)*
No Rooms: *18 En suite 18*		*Dinner £45.00*
TV in Rooms. *Yes*	**Location:**	*Leave A85 at Taynuilt to B845*
Room Tel. *Yes* **Disabled:** *Dining only*		*through village of Kilchrenan to the*
Children: *Yes* **Pets:** *By arrangement*		*Lochside*

CREEL RESTAURANT WITH ROOMS

Front Road, St. Margaret's Hope, Orkney. KW17 2SL
Tel: 01856 831311
Email: creelorkney@btinternet.com www.thecreel.co.uk

Although not quite on your doorstep this is a mecca for all who enjoy food prepared to consistently high standards on the south part of Orkney just over the Churchill Barriers and 14 miles from Kirkwall. Took the Gillsbay Ferry directly to St. Margaret's Hope and a short drive to the 'restaurant with rooms'. Alternatively there is a ferry from Scrabster. Proprietor chef Alan Craigie and his wife Joyce (front of house) are 'well kent faces' and enjoy a fine reputation for their cuisine (27th season). There is complete dedication here - food prepared using much of the island produce but with originality, flair and imagination that reflect a high quality of culinary skills. It could be described as modern cooking with a hint of Orcadian influence. The Creel has 2 AA red rosettes and is rated highly in the Good Food Guide (UK). A bit of an adventure getting there but an experience not to be missed. **AA** 🏵🏵 🍴

Open: *Closed Jan/Feb. and Mon. Open*	**Disabled:**	*Unsuitable*
Apr-Sept & weekends Nov/Dec	**Covers:**	*34*
	Price Guide:	*B/B single from £65.00*
No Rooms: *3 En Suite*		*B/B double from £110.00*
TV in Rooms: *Yes* **Room Tel.** *No*		*Dinner £32.50 - £39.50*
Children: *Over 5*	**Location:** *A961 South across Churchill barriers. 20 mins from Kirkwall*	

THE HORSESHOE INN

Eddleston Village, Edinburgh Road, Nr. Peebles. EH45 8QP

Tel: 01721 730225

Email: reservations@horseshoeinn.co.uk   www.horseshoeinn.co.uk

One of my old 'stomping grounds' in the 1970's. Remembered by many with great affection I am pleased to see it getting back to what it was all about. A great welcome to all (sadly lacking before) and good wholesome food at a reasonable cost. Also the friendly ambience has returned where staff take a genuine interest in their guests. It will take time – however, off to a fine start with sensible bistro (and daily specials) and a la carte menus expertly prepared by head chef Riad Peerbux. 2 AA rosettes reflects dedication, sound technical skills with sophisticated and appropriate garnishes. Choice of informal or more formal dining depending on the occasion. Good wine cellar at affordable prices. Great location on the main Edinburgh road south between the capital and Peebles. There are 8 delightful rooms at the rear of the restaurant – ideal for those that prefer to stay out of Edinburgh on the periphery with ample car parking. I have enjoyed my 2 visits here and as General Manager Mark Slaney told me, "we welcome everyone here – even if it's just for a cup of coffee!" Go for it – once you have been you will return.**AA** 🏵🏵 🍷

Open: *All year*		**Price Guide:** *Rooms £50.00 B&B pppn*	
No Rooms: 8		*Bistro £9.50 - £20.00*	
TV in Rooms: *Yes*		*A la carte £40.00*	
Room Tel. *Yes*	**Disabled:** *Dining only*	**Location:**	
Children: *Yes*	**Covers:** 36	*20 mls south of Edinburgh on A703, 5 mls north of Peebles*	

63 TAY STREET

63 Tay Street, Perth. PH2 8NN

Tel: 01738 441451

Email: info@63taystreet.com   www.63taystreet.com

Now officially the City of Perth, 63 Tay Street has a great location overlooking the famous River Tay and close to the main shopping area. 'Local, honest, simple' are the words used at the top of the dinner menu and this fine dining establishment is the domain of talented chef/patron Graeme Pallister. Had 4 visits this year – Graeme uses the natural agricultural and maritime resources from the rich pastures and rivers of Perthshire. Seasonal menus offer honest fayre, uncomplicated dishes with great taste. Vibrant flavours. Risotto of Scottish crab, home-smoked pork ribeye and a chocolate souffle could be your choice. Four course restricted lunch menu and an excellent pre-theatre dinner at £17.95! Good wine list to boot. Great ambience - contemporary with wooden floors and quality clothed tables. Service faultless. A wonderful dining experience which reflects a consistent top end 2 AA red rosette award. Also linked to The Parklands Hotel at St. Leonard's Bank in Perth where Graeme supervises the food operation. (See separate entry within the hotel book). Highly recommended.**AA** 🏵🏵 🍷

Open: *All year ex. Sun & Mon*	**Covers:**	32
No Rooms: *N/A*	**Price Guide:**	*Dinner £37.00 (5 course)*
TV in Rooms: *N/A* **Room Tel.** *N/A*		*Lunch £25.00 (4 course)*
Children: *Over 10 for dinner*		*Pre-Theatre Dinner £17.95*
Disabled: *Yes*	**Location:**	*63 Tay Street, beside the river*

APRON STAGE RESTAURANT

5 King's Street, Stanley, Perth. PH1 4ND
Tel: 01738 828888
Email: info@apronstagerestaurant.co.uk www.apronstagerestaurant.co.uk

Idyllic intimate country restaurant in the attractive village of Stanley just north of Perth. Unusually small for a restaurant (maximum covers of 18) and the kitchen is tiny. It was good to catch up with well known chef Tony Heath and partner Shona Drysdale who have been here since 2006. I had first met Tony in 1988 when he worked in a local Perthshire hotel and have followed his career over the last 24 years. Don't be deceived by the restricted menu, opening times and space. With sound prep work allied with the talents of Tony and Shona the food served here is of a very high standard. Clear well defined flavours using good quality ingredients. New season Glamis asparagus, breast of guinea fowl with twice cooked spiced pork belly and a mouth watering pudding could be your choice. Good cheese board option and wine to complement a good meal. Jane completes the 'team' and works wonders with the 'front of house' operation. Private parties by arrangement – reservations for dinner advisable. Lunch only on a Friday. Relaxed and friendly atmosphere – great ambience.

Open: *Dinner: Wed-Sat; Lunch: Friday only*		**Price Guide:**	*Lunch £13.75 (2 course); £21.75 (3 course)*
No Rooms: *N/A*			*Dinner £25.00 - £28.00*
TV in Rooms: *N/A*	**Room Tel.** *N/A*	**Location:**	*1 mile north of Perth on A9, take slip road*
Children: *Over 8*			*signposted Stanley. King's Street is just off*
Disabled: *Yes*	**Covers:** *18 (max)*		*the main road through village*

RESTAURANT@THE ROSEDALE

Beaumont Crescent, Portree, Isle of Skye IV51 9DF
Tel : 01478 613131   Fax : 01478 612531
Email : robertmacaskill@hotmail.co.uk www.portreerestaurant.co.uk

Located within The Rosedale Hotel overlooking the harbour this is 'the place to eat' when visiting Portree. After a lot of hard work (and worry!) Robert Macaskill is forging ahead and making a name for himself. Ideal location with stunning views from the restaurant over Portree Bay. Sampled his skills once again and he is absolutely passionate about his food. Sourcing quality ingredients not a problem and known already by his suppliers. Menus are simple with good choice. Seafood a speciality. Flavours were evident and my meal cooked to perfection. Sound technical skills on display. Not fine dining but a really good meal and value for money. Service was excellent – the popular and well known Willie Shankie (front of house) appears to be everywhere at the one time! During the 'busy time' in the Summer only open for dinner to make sure diners' expectations are fully met. Although well known locally The Restaurant@The Rosedale will become known as a food destination for many.

Open: *All year except Nov-mid March.*	**Disabled:**	*Not suitable*
No Rooms: *N/A*	**Covers:**	*36*
TV in Rooms: *N/A*	**Price Guide:**	*Dinner £20.00 - £30.00 (from 5.30pm)*
Room Tel. *N/A*	**Location:**	*Harbour overlooking Portree Bay*
Children: *Yes*		

CRAIG MILLAR @ 16 WEST END

16 West End, St. Monans, Fife. KY10 2BX
Tel: 01333 730327
Email: craigmillar@16westend.com www.16westend.com

Once again a most enjoyable dining experience at this famous fish restaurant in Fife. Known by reputation, Craig Millar has transformed this restaurant to one of the best in this area of Scotland. Over the 21 years I have known Craig he has developed his skills and a visit here is a must for the discerning diner. Idyllic location overlooking the harbour of this famous fishing village. Great ambience from within – intimate bar with fire leads through to the main restaurant where the views are quite spectacular. Menus are fairly restricted (which indicates good preping and sourcing of ingredients) with fish dishes prevalent. My main choice of cod (once again!) was just perfect. Good combinations, depth of flavour and taste evident. Home made breads and petit fours were outstanding. Tasting menu available for a complete table – otherwise choice of courses for lunch and dinner plus a set menu for lunch (£18:00) Wine cellar of note. Service faultless. Don't miss this one out when visiting the Fife area. Highly recommended. *AA* ❀ ❀

Open: All year ex. Mon. & Tues.		Price Guide:	Dinner: £35.00 - £45.00; Lunch: £22.00 - £26.00
No Rooms: N/A			Tasting Menu: £55.00; With wine: £80.00
TV in Rooms: N/A Room Tel. N/A			Set Lunch: £18.00
Children: Over 5 Disabled: Yes		Location:	Enter village from A917 from St.Andrews/
Covers: 45			Anstruther. Down to harbour and turn right.

DEANES

36-40 Howard Street, Belfast. BT1 6PF
Tel: 02890 331134
Email: info@michaeldeane.co.uk www.michaeldeane.co.uk

Although the main fine dining experience remains in Howard Street, Michael Deane has expanded his 'empire' considerably over the years. These include a bar and grill at College Gardens, a deli store at Banbridge and a restaurant and seafood bar at Queens. A great success story from the time I met him in Scotland in 1988. His exhuberant style - both of showmanship and of uncompromisingly perfectionist cooking has elicited praise from the sternest of food critics and the most demanding food guides. Since 2010 Michael has changed his menus to reflect a more 'down to earth' approach and can now be classified as more Irish traditional with a hint of French influence. Specialist suppliers and great prep work here - food produced to a very high standard. From his beginnings at Claridges Michael has been on a pilgrimage - always propelled by his pure passion for food and its possibilities. 3 AA food rosettes since 1997. Keep this one in mind and follow this entry whenever in Belfast. *AA* ❀ ❀ ❀

Open: Closed Sun.-Tues.		Disabled:	Brasserie only
No Rooms: N/A		Covers:	35
TV in Rooms: N/A Room Tel. N/A		Price Guide:	Dinner: £65.00 (2 courses) - £80.00
Children: Welcome			Lunch: Brasserie - from £20.00

Pan Roast Quail, Confit Leg Bon Bon
And Foie Gras Mousse

(serves 4)

Ingredients:

Quail

Whole quail x 4
Duck fat x 1L
Prunes x 4
Walnuts x 4
Pear x 1
Quail egg

Carrot Purée

Carrots x 200g
Chicken stk x 200ml
Star anise x 1
Butter x 10g
Cream x 20ml

Leg bon bon

Confit legs x 8
Red onion jam 10g
Jus x 10ml
Parsley 2g
Salt and pepper
Pane mix

Foie Gras Mousse

Sliced rouge foie gras x 8 pieces
Cognac x 50ml
Salt and pepper
Nutmeg
Sugar
Cream x 100ml
Ground candied walnuts

Sauce

Quail carcases
Madeira
Mirepoix
Dark chicken stock

Method:

Marinate the sliced foie gras overnight in the cognac, salt, pepper, nutmeg and sugar. Prepare the quail by removing the legs, and taking the breast off the crown, reserving carcases for sauce. Confit the legs in the duck fat for 1 hour 15 minutes at 130 degrees. Finely slice the carrots and cook in the chicken stock and add the star anise. When the carrots are soft and the stock is reduced, remove the star anise and blitz in the food processor with the cream and butter. Pass and keep warm.

For the sauce, roast the carcases until golden brown, add the mirepoix and deglaze with Madeira. Add chicken stock and simmer until reduced by ¾; then pass through muslin and Monte with butter. Remove the marinated foie gras from the fridge and pan fry on both sides. Place in the food processor and blitz until smooth. Semi whip the cream and fold through the foie gras and chill; check seasoning. While still warm, carefully pick the meat from the legs into a bowl, reserving the bones for garnish. Add the red onion jam, parsley and jus, season and roll into a sausage shape. Place in freezer until well chilled and, once chilled cut into 10 gram portions and pane in the mix.

To Serve:

Heat a sauté pan with rapeseed oil, place the breast skin side down, season and cook for approx 1½ minutes until the skin is golden. Turn over and cook for a further minute. Rest the meat on a tray. Shallow fry the bon bon. To assemble, place the carrot purée on the left side of the plate and drag with a spoon to the other side. Place the bon bon in the centre of the plate with the reserved quail leg bone popping out. Trim the breast and place either side of the bon bon. With a hot spoon Roche the foie gras and roll in the ground walnuts, placing at one end of the plate. At the opposite side place half a deep fried quail egg. Scatter the bronoise of prune and shards of pear, garnish with pea friss and drizzle the quail jus over.

Head Chef: Scott Scorer
Ballathie House, Kinclaven
(also see entry page 47)

Miso and Honey-glazed Salmon Darne with Aparagus, Young Garlic and Shaved Horseradish

(serves 4)

Ingredients:

1 head young garlic or 2 garlic scapes
500g asparagus, trimmed
2 teaspoons freshly grated horseradish root
1 tablespoon olive oil
Half a lemon sliced into 4 wedges

2 tablespoons yellow miso paste
5 tablespoons sake wine
5 tablespoons mirin
2 1/2 teaspoons ginger grated
1 tablespoon light honey
20ml rapeseed oil
4 skinless salmon darns 6oz each

Method:

Whisk the miso, sake, mirin, ginger, honey, and oil together in a large bowl. Add the salmon darns and coat with the marinade. Cover and refrigerate for 24 hours.

Wipe any excess marinade from the salmon fillets and place them on a baking tray. Place the dish on the top shelf of a preheated oven at 240°C and cook until the top of the fish is nicely browned: 3-4 minutes. Then move the dish to the centre rack and bake until the salmon is cooked - depending on size about 4 minutes. Set aside to cool.

Trim the root end of the garlic and wash. Cut it 4 inches from the bulb, then slice the bulb and stem lengthwise through the middle. Remove any tough outer skin. Lay each half cut-side-down and slice as thinly as possible (if using garlic scapes, also slice as thinly as possible). Gather up the garlic in a bowl, season with salt and work the salt into the sliced garlic using your fingers. This mellows the flavor a little. Sit for at least 10 minutes.

Cut asparagus into ¼ inch pieces on the diagonal. Heat a frying pan and cook the asparagus for 2 minutes in a drizzle of oil. Arrange the asparagus on individual plates. Sprinkle the sliced garlic over the asparagus, drizzle with some of the rapeseed oil. Using a vegetable peeler, scrape away the horseradish skin from the root and give it a rinse. Grate the root over the asparagus: about 2 teaspoons of horseradish. Season with more salt if needed, place the salmon on top of the asparagus and serve with lemon wedges.

Head Chef: Mark De Freitas
Lake Hotel and Restaurant, Aberfoyle
(also see entry page 19)

Loin and Slow Cooked Featherblade of Royal Deeside Beef, Potato and Horseradish Pancake, with Roasted Roots

Ingredients:

4 x 3oz pieces Beef Loin (centre cut, minimum 28 days aged)
600g beef featherblade

2 carrots	8 peppercorns
3 shallots	3 juniper berries
1 stick celery	1 litre good quality beef stock
½ leek	200ml red wine
2 bay leaves	20g red currant jelly
1 star anise	3 garlic cloves

Method:

Featherblade:
Seal featherblade in a hot pan with a little oil; when coloured remove. In the same pan, roast chopped shallots, carrots, celery and leek. Add spices, wine, stock and jelly. Bring to boil, add beef featherblade, cover and place in oven at 160°C for 3 hours or until tender. Allow to cool slightly in cooking juices, remove while still warm and roll tightly in cling film, refrigerate until cold and slice into 4 portions. Strain braising stock and reduce by ⅔. To serve, warm featherblade in stock, serve with gravy.

For the Fillets:
Season and sear the fillets in a hot pan until well coloured. Place in a hot oven (190°C) for 5 minutes. Rest for 8 minutes, carve and serve.

Potato and Horseradish Pancake Ingredients:

400g mashed potatoes (still warm)	1 tbsp horseradish sauce
2 egg yolks	1 tsp chopped fresh parsley
2 egg whites (whisked to still peaks)	1 chopped button shallot
50g clarified butter	Salt and pepper
50g plain flour	

Method:

Place all ingredients expect the egg whites in a bowl and mix well (do not overwork or the potatoes will become gluey). Fold in egg whites, ⅓ at a time. Cook pancakes in rapeseed oil or butter in blini pans.

To Serve:

Serve with roasted root vegetables, shallots and seasonal mushrooms. Drizzle with the red meat braising stock.

Head Chef: David Littlewood
Raemoir House Hotel, Banchory
(also see entry page 17)

Grilled West Coast Mackerel: Smoked Mackerel, Beetroot and Compressed Cucumber

Smoked Mackerel Pate

Take 1 whole smoked mackerel and flake the flesh carefully checking for bones, then set aside. Whisk to soft peak 75ml of double cream, to the mackerel add 25g of horseradish sauce and 30g of crème fraiche, some chopped parsley and a pinch of ground white pepper. Place into blender and pulse blend a few times to roughly combine, then once combined fold in the whipped cream and adjust seasoning with a squeeze of lime juice and salt if needed.

Beetroot Relish

Grate 2 large raw beetroot on a fine grater. In a pan cover the beetroot with 100ml of red wine vinegar, 100ml of port and 100g of Light Brown Sugar. In some muslin cloth add 2 cloves, 1 star anise and 2 bay leaves then add this to the beetroot. Cook out on a low heat until the beetroot loses some of its bite and the cooking liquor has reduced.

Beetroot Gel

Take 200ml of fresh Beetroot Juice and place in a pan, gently warm and season with sugar and salt. Weigh out 2.5g of agar agar and mix with a pinch of caster sugar, then bring the beetroot juice quickly to the boil. Whisk in the agar mix, boil for one minute and then set aside in a container and chill until set hard. Once set hard roughly chop and put into liquidiser. Blend until reconstituted into a purée consistency.

Pickled Beetroot Rings

Take 1 raw Beetroot and 1 Raw Golden Beetroot, slice them 1mm thin on a mandolin then cut small rings with a cutter and set aside. For the pickle bring to boil 100ml of distilled vinegar, 100ml of water , 80g of caster sugar, 2 bay leaves and a few juniper berries. Once boiled leave to cool and infuse. Once pickle solution has cooled split evenly and pour over the cut beetroot cold. (As it is so finely cut you want to keep some freshness to the beetroot).

Compressed Cucumber Dressing

Take 1 cucumber and peel with a vegetable peeler. Split in half with a knife and remove centre seeds with a parisiene scoop. Then vac pac the cucumber flesh on as high a setting as the machine shall allow to remove any unnecessary air within the cucumber flesh. Leave over night to set. Chop a few fronds of Bronze fennel, squeeze half a lemon, and add to this 50ml of good quality extra virgin olive oil. Then take your cucumber and dice into small cubes, add to your dressing base and season with salt if needed.

Head Chef: Max Hogg
Livingstons Restaurant, Linlithgow, West Lothian
(also see entry page 78)

Lightly fried Aromatic Duck Egg, Ham Mousse and Pea Shoots

Ham Mousse:

200g finest cooked ham finely diced
200g white roux lightly seasoned
100ml lightly whipped cream
1 sheet of gelatine
Sherry
Paprika
Cayenne Pepper
Salt

Method:

Soften gelatine in cold water, squeeze and dissolve in 2 tablespoons of warm sherry, in a blender place ham, roux and gelatine and blend till smooth, remove to a bowl and gently fold in cream, season to taste with sherry, Paprika, salt and the cayenne leave to set in fridge for at least 2 hours.

Tomato Vinaigrette:

1 ripe tomato, skinned, deseeded and diced
1 red chilli, blackened, skinned and finely diced
½ red pepper, blackened, skinned and finely diced
1 teaspoon of salted capers, rinsed and dried
2 tablespoons of quality olive oil
1 dessertspoonful of cabernet sauvignon vinegar

Combine all ingredients, season to taste, reserve.

To serve:

4 duck eggs
3 tablespoons of clarified butter
50g fresh pea shoots
A selection of equal quantities of roasted spice seeds
1 teaspoon of a vanilla sugar syrup or maple syrup

Method:

Warm the butter in a non-stick pan and cook egg to your liking, lightly season once cooked and place on a warmed plate, add vinaigrette to egg, seeds and dot of syrup on yolk, quenelle of ham mousse with hot spoons and top with peas shoots, serve immediately.

Chef/Patron: Graeme Pallister
63 Tay Street, Perth
(also see entry page 81)

STEVENSONS

SCOTLAND'S
GOOD HOTEL AND FOOD BOOK
2013

Order Form: **Alan Stevenson Publications**
Fala, 20 West Cairn Crescent, Penicuik,
Midlothian EH26 0AR
Tel: 01968 678015
E-mail: alan@stevensons-scotland.com

Date: .... Please mail .... Copies of
Stevensons, Scotland's Good Hotel and Food Book, 2013.

Your Name: ....

Address: ....

.... Postcode: ....

Retail Price
(All prices include postage and packaging)

United Kingdom	**£12.00**
Europe	**£16.00**
Euro Zone	**€24.00**
Outside Europe	**£20.00**
USA only	**$28.00**
Canada only	**$30.00**

Alternatively purchase online at www.stevensons-scotland.com
Multiple orders: price on application
Orders outwith the UK consigned by airmail
Payment in pounds sterling payable to Alan Stevenson Publications

No. of Copies: ...... at £/$/€ .... each. Total £/$/€ ....

I enclose a Cheque/Bank Draft   Total £/$/€ ....

Hotels continued

Restaurants listed alphabetically by name

INDEX

Hotels listed alphabetically by name

See contents page 4 for list of Trade Sponsors.